USS *Midway*

AMERICA'S SHIELD

SCOTT McGAUGH

PELICAN PUBLISHING COMPANY
Gretna 2011

Copyright © 2011
By Scott McGaugh
All rights reserved

*The word "Pelican" and the depiction of a pelican are
trademarks of Pelican Publishing Company, Inc., and are
registered in the U.S. Patent and Trademark Office.*

Library of Congress Cataloging-in-Publication Data

McGaugh, Scott.
 USS Midway : America's shield / by Scott McGaugh.
    p. cm.
 Includes index.
  ISBN 978-1-58980-896-6 (pbk. : alk. paper) 1. Midway (Attack aircraft
carrier) I. Title.
 VA65.M56M34 2011
 359.9'435—dc22

                              2011011876

Printed in the United States of America

Published by Pelican Publishing Company, Inc.
1000 Burmaster Street, Gretna, Louisiana 70053

To my son, Garrett,
the inspiration to make
my life as worthy and meaningful as possible

The USS *Midway* became famous for marathon deployments that sometimes took it into very rough seas. Occasionally, forty-foot waves threatened to wash over a flight deck that was fifty feet above the water.

Contents

Every deployment carried risk and danger. Months spent away from family and friends were both stressful and a threat to crew morale. However, that same duty made every homecoming a cherished one.

Preface

The year I turned eighteen, I faced the prospect of giving up two years of my life if my country ordered me to join the military. As the Vietnam War raged, our nation's military was based on a mandatory draft of young men to serve in uniform. Each year they were selected randomly by lottery, according to their birth dates. Those who were ordered to serve had no choice but to report for active duty, join the military reserve, or apply for a student deferment.

When it was our turn, most of my friends and I simply hoped we would not be chosen. A few volunteered for military service so they could have a limited choice of assignments. I was not drafted. I continued my education, got married, and went on with my life.

Over the years, I have thought about some of my classmates who died in the jungles of Vietnam, less than a year after graduating from high school. As I got older, some of the stories from those who survived brought me chills and even tears.

Over time, I grew to admire all the young men and women who serve their country in uniform, particularly when our nation is divided over whether we should send troops overseas to a faraway war. That requires a strength of conviction and courage that I hope I have somewhere inside me, too. I also grew to cherish my freedom and the American way of life that they defend, sometimes with their lives.

In 1996 I began volunteering to help bring the retired USS

Midway aircraft carrier to my hometown of San Diego to become a naval aviation museum. I saw it as an opportunity to say "thank you" to those who serve. What I thought would be a few months of volunteering turned into eight years. It became both the mission and passion of my life to help create a museum, tribute, and memorial to those who make America and freedom possible.

When the USS *Midway* opened as a museum in June 2004, I became the marketing director. By that time I had interviewed hundreds of *Midway* sailors, pilots, and officers. I wrote the first book on the history of the USS *Midway*, *Midway Magic*, based on those interviews and then published a collection of USS *Midway* historical and museum photographs, called *Midway Memories*.

USS Midway: *America's Shield* contains the largest collection published to date of rarely seen *Midway* photographs. I hope readers find it as inspirational as I was humbled when I interviewed many of the men who forged this remarkable piece of American history.

It continues to be an honor and a privilege for me to help preserve their legacy for future generations.

Acknowledgments

The preservation of irreplaceable history always requires a team effort. Since 2004, more than fifteen thousand individuals have come together to maintain the legacy of the USS *Midway*. They have supported and worked to restore this historic aircraft carrier and convert it into the nation's most-visited ship museum. Their tireless and selfless dedication in preserving this history made *USS* Midway: *America's Shield* possible.

The inspirational leadership of retired rear admiral Mac McLaughlin as president and chief executive officer of the museum has galvanized employees, hundreds of volunteers, and thousands of supporters. Every day their mission is to preserve the historic USS *Midway* and the legacy of those who serve, to inspire and educate future generations, and to entertain museum guests. Their vision is that the USS Midway Museum will become America's living symbol of freedom.

The historic, archival, and exhibit teams led by Duke Windsor, Rudy Shappee, Karl Zingheim, Bill Coleman, David Hanson, and others have assembled the nation's most complete array of archival, oral history, artifact, and documentary collections about the USS *Midway*. Teams of unsung restoration volunteers work in spaces deep inside the ship, knowing they someday will be open to the public and add to the USS *Midway* legacy. Much of this archival and restoration work forms the foundation of *USS* Midway: *America's Shield*.

11

The USS Midway Museum's remarkable volunteer corps also is responsible for preserving so much of the history that is reflected in this book. Volunteer director Laurie Switzer manages more than seven hundred volunteers, who contribute more than 175,000 hours annually. The museum's docent leaders, Jim Nash, Frank Hudson, and Kristine Hayes, are responsible for hundreds of volunteer docents, some of them former USS *Midway* sailors, pilots, and officers who share their experiences with museum guests.

The museum's education department hosts more than forty thousand K-12 students annually on study trips aboard, focusing on real-life math, science, social studies, history, and even citizenship. Led by Sara Hanscom, Wayne Nuzzolo, John Rosas, and others, the USS Midway Museum's education team was indispensible in helping me understand how to present this story.

The creation of a floating museum has been made possible by the dedication of Charles Gordon and Vic Zambrano and their teams who are responsible for overcoming the preservation and maintenance challenges of an aircraft carrier built more than half a century ago. Bobby Reyes similarly leads a dedicated corps of aircraft restoration volunteers.

Yet as vital as the work of the museum teams has been, I cannot begin to adequately express my thanks to more than five hundred former *Midway* sailors, pilots, and officers who graciously shared their stories in personal interviews. Sometimes they revealed aspects of their life in the military that they had never felt comfortable sharing with their families. Some of those experiences grabbed me by the throat and made me realize how lucky we are to have so many men and women willing to volunteer for military service today.

Rudy Shappee and former public-affairs officer Joe Ciokon, both of whom made the Navy their careers, continue to be exceedingly generous with their time in helping me understand what it was like serving America aboard ship thousands of miles from home. Countless other museum employees and legions of volunteers all are contributing to preserving the legacy of the USS *Midway* for all of America.

Finally, my agent, Neil Salkind, and the Pelican Publishing Company team of Nina Kooij, Suzanne Pfefferle, John Scheyd, Caitlin Smith, and others all played greatly appreciated roles in getting this book into your hands.

It is my honor to offer *USS* Midway: *America's Shield* as a tribute to the legacy of those who serve America as well as a source of inspiration and education for generations to come.

Introduction

In 1945, the USS *Midway* first headed to sea with thousands of young men aboard. It returned to port for the final time forty-seven years later. All told, more than 200,000 young Americans had sailed on the longest-serving U.S. Navy aircraft carrier of the twentieth century. For nearly fifty years, the crew, whose average age was nineteen, had participated in some of the most important and influential events of world affairs.

USS Midway: *America's Shield* is the true story of these young sailors, most of whom were only a few years past high school. It is the story of sons of dairy farmers, steel-mill workers, albacore fishermen, and watchmakers from Albany, Columbus, Los Angeles, and Austin.

This also is a story of empowerment. It is a narrative of young adults playing seemingly small but critical roles and contributing to larger missions that influenced world affairs. Most of these young men spent less than two years aboard *Midway*, assigned seemingly impossible responsibility and learning that training, trust, and teamwork enabled them to shape events that defined the latter half of the twentieth century.

It is a narrative that blends individual responsibility with unfathomable circumstances at sea. *USS* Midway: *America's Shield* is a collective biography of thousands of young heroes who came of age thousands of miles from home.

Their voyage began in the turbulence following World War II and continued through the Cold War and the beginning of the War on Terror. *USS* Midway: *America's Shield* is personalized history, and that is the most compelling history of all.

Chapter 1

Coming of Age

The world was at war in 1943. America fought Germany to the east and Japan to the west. Although the tide of battle had begun to turn in the Americans' favor, the outcome was far from certain. Aircraft and ship construction was a top national priority. On October 27, work began in a Virginia shipyard on the USS Midway, an aircraft carrier that would become the largest and most sophisticated warship in the world. Construction continued twenty-four hours a day in a race to get Midway into the war.

Meanwhile, the life path of millions of American boys in high school in 1943 was clearly marked. Within a year or two, they would be fighting for their country, whether they wanted to or not. During World War II, a senior in high school could volunteer for the military before he finished his final semester and still receive his high-school degree. He could be as young as seventeen and still volunteer, with his parents' permission. By volunteering, he could choose the Navy, Army, or Marines. Or he could wait to be drafted and have no choice as to where he would be assigned. A young man's life in 1943 was decided by others. He knew he could be sent to fight and was expected to die if necessary.

It might be on a tiny Pacific atoll such as Tarawa, smaller than New York City's Central Park. It might be in the snow-laden forests of France, where men lost blackened fingers to frostbite. He could be assigned to a unit chasing Germans across the North African desert. It might be aboard a submarine that hunted the enemy from deep in the frigid North Atlantic Ocean.

Construction of the USS *Midway* continued around the clock in order to enter World War II. Built in only seventeen months at a cost of $90 million, it became the largest and most powerful ship in the world, but it missed the war by one week.

More than eleven million teenagers were drafted into military service in World War II, in addition to the six million who volunteered. Battle hardened those who survived. Some came of age aboard the USS Midway aircraft carrier when it was ready for sea duty. They became part of an unprecedented forty-seven-year odyssey beginning on September 10, 1945. Their orders were to preserve a newfound fragile peace.

Buddy Herrmann's hands ached as he held onto the USS *Midway* aircraft carrier's brass steering wheel in the darkened pilothouse. The young sailor, who usually had duty in one of the carrier's anti-aircraft gun turrets, was temporarily assigned to stand night watch at

World War II's exposed aircraft engines posed unique challenges when the USS *Midway* sailed into sub-Arctic water. The oil in the engines had to remain heated overnight so crews could start the planes when air operations were scheduled.

the helm in the island high above the flight deck. Darkness blanketed *Midway* as sixty-knot winds drove rolling mountains of waves into its side. Each wave's attack threatened to spin the wheel free of his grip and throw Herrmann against nearby equipment. Bruised and battered, he leaned hard into one thundering wave after another through the night.

Down on the hangar deck where *Midway*'s planes were repaired and parked, each ship's roll threw men off their feet. They bounced on the nonskid surface, scraping arms, legs, and faces. Some broke fingers when they tried to keep from falling. Sailors on the hangar deck nearly lost their balance every few seconds as the ship rolled

Men working on the flight deck off the coast of Greenland faced permanent frostbite injuries during a daring operation called "Operation Frostbite" in 1946. The USS *Midway* was the first carrier to operate extensively in the midwinter sub-Arctic.

with the waves. It was 1946, and the Labrador Sea near Greenland threatened to pound the life out of *Midway*.

Four years earlier, when most of *Midway*'s crew still attended high school, Pres. Franklin Delano Roosevelt had faced a huge decision in December 1942. It had been six months since the American Navy had inflicted a stunning defeat on the Japanese in a sea battle near Midway Atoll in World War II. The Navy had broken the Japanese communication code, which enabled it to spring a trap on a powerful fleet of Japanese warships. Had the enemy seized Midway, Japan would have been in a position to attack Hawaii and threaten the continental United States. But the Americans prevailed and the tide of war in the Pacific turned in their favor.

America still faced a massive battlefield across the Pacific Ocean, however. Should the president authorize faster construction of dozens of small, escort aircraft carriers with limited capability or approve a huge, new kind of aircraft carrier that would dwarf everything afloat and transport more than one hundred aircraft into battle? If the enemy somehow sank that kind of ship, it could become a devastating Navy loss.

After many discussions in the White House and Pentagon, President Roosevelt decided to build the largest, most powerful ship the world had ever known. It was named the USS *Midway* in honor of America's victory at Midway Atoll. Shipyard welders, electricians, plumbers, steamfitters, and others were assembled to work seven days a week to get *Midway* into the war as soon as possible.

Meanwhile, Dudley Gilbert in Rhode Island, John Rieman in Missouri, Donald Fry in Pennsylvania, and Don Struchen in Iowa were freshmen or sophomores in high school. They had no idea that in a few short years they would help launch a ship on an odyssey that would continue for an unparalleled forty-seven years.

Newport News Shipbuilding & Dry Dock Company in Virginia received a $90 million contract to build the USS *Midway*. Work got under way on October 27, 1943. Within a few months, the 29,000-ton hull took shape as shipyard workers pored over ninety tons of blueprints in an era long before computer-aided designs.

They worked continuously to assemble the Navy's first steel flight deck on *Midway*. (Earlier aircraft-carrier flight decks made of wood had proved vulnerable to attacks by suicide Japanese dive bombers.) Welders joined together a 196,000-piece flight-deck jigsaw puzzle.

Some pieces weighed several tons and others as little as a pound. Once they completed the flight deck, workers assembled eight, 650-square-foot wooden houses on the deck to protect the welders as they worked through the night. A small city of thousands of shipyard workers toiled around the clock for almost eighteen months, eager to get the USS *Midway* into the war.

By March 1945, the USS *Midway* shipyard workers were ready to slide the nearly finished *Midway* from its dry dock and into the water for the first time. Called the "christening," the centuries-old ritual of slamming a full champagne bottle against its bow was watched by

When the USS *Midway* was commissioned in 1945, it became the largest ship in the world for a decade and the first U.S. Navy ship too large for the Panama Canal (five feet too wide).

thousands. A daring pilot who had survived the Battle of Midway, Ensign George Gay, was a guest of honor. Speakers urged the audience to buy war bonds to help pay for the war and in honor of the world's most sophisticated aircraft carrier.

When completed and commissioned six months later on September 10, *Midway* became the first U.S. Navy ship too wide for the Panama Canal. It was a floating steel honeycomb of 1,750 watertight rooms, called compartments in the Navy. The small compartments made the carrier less vulnerable to flooding from torpedo damage. Four turbines fed by twelve boilers were spread throughout the ship to improve survivability. Although that made it difficult to work on them, they produced 212,000 horsepower. *Midway*'s top speed was thirty-three knots, fast enough for a sailor to water-ski behind an aircraft carrier that weighed 90 million pounds.

Midway's final construction phase came at a time when America was slowly winning the war in both Europe and the Pacific. The battle for a small Pacific island called Iwo Jima had raged for nearly a month. But victory remained uncertain. America continued drafting young men for military duty. Many decided to enlist before they received a draft notice, so they could choose the Navy, Marines, Army, or Army's Air Force. From every corner of America they were sent to basic-training camps.

Joe Delaney hated living with his divorced father in Waltham, Massachusetts while his brother and sister lived with his mother in New York. He was seventeen years old in 1944 and miserable. He talked his father into allowing him to enlist in the Navy. Joe was sure he would be fighting the Japanese a few months later. He was trained to be a communications specialist.

Ray Shirley spent most of his boyhood in Tennessee and northern Georgia. After graduating high school, he spent two years behind a mule and a plow or handpicking cotton in hot and humid summers on the family farm. He decided there had to be a better way to make a living. He volunteered for the naval air corps. After training, he was responsible for taking care of bombs.

After growing up in a Missouri orphanage, John Rieman enlisted as soon as he turned seventeen, about the same time that construction got under way on the USS *Midway* in 1943. The Navy sent him to North Africa and he became a cook.

The son of a watch adjuster in rural Connecticut, Buddy Herrmann enlisted and left a family so poor they had to hunt ducks in the fall and fish in the summer to put food on their table. In the absence of a refrigerator, they had Jell-O only in the winter, when it was cold enough for his mother put it outside on a windowsill so it could thicken. Herrmann would learn how to fire the anti-aircraft guns that were installed around the edge of *Midway*'s flight deck.

The reasons varied for others who enlisted and ultimately were assigned to *Midway*. "It was just the right thing to do. Everyone else was joining up and by enlisting I had a choice of what service I'd serve in," said one sailor. Some decided early in life that the Navy was for them.

Others were more calculating. "You couldn't get a date unless you joined the service," said Tom Turner, a Marine on *Midway*. Turner enlisted in the summer of 1944. After flunking out of a military foreign-language school, he would be trained to fire *Midway*'s anti-aircraft guns.

Then the world changed. In the span of four days in August 1945, two nuclear bombs destroyed Japan's will to wage war. In the time it took to split an atom, the operational plan for *Midway* and its crew mutated. They would not fight the Japanese as they had expected. *Midway*'s mission became one of preserving a peace that had been won at a cost of more than one million dead and wounded American men and women by the end of World War II.

Leaving home to join the Navy and see the world also included hard work, such as keeping 1,750 rooms aboard the USS *Midway* clean. Some members of the crew were permanently assigned to ship's maintenance, deep below the water line.

A month later, thousands of men rode trains destined for Newport, Rhode Island. They had been told they were part of the first USS *Midway* crew. They were to become "plankowners," a title and maritime honor dating back to the era of wooden sailing ships. The original crewmembers of all ships were called plankowners. About three thousand men became *Midway*'s "ship's company"—the crew that ran the ship. Each had a specific job.

Dudley Gilbert would help operate the four, twenty-ton anchors and hundreds of feet of anchor chain, each link weighing 130 pounds. He had joined the Navy because it seemed everyone he knew was either in the military or working for a defense contractor. He felt that it was his obligation to enlist when the country was at war. Don Struchen would join Tom Turner and Buddy Herrmann at the anti-aircraft guns. The Iowa farm boy didn't pass aviation radioman school so he was assigned to the guns. John Rieman would find himself in one of six kitchens, called galleys, aboard *Midway*. And Ray Shirley would report to the weapons department to help handle thousands of tons of bombs, including some classified as secret, and ammunition stored deep inside the aircraft carrier.

Another 1,500 young men represented *Midway*'s "air wing." They were the pilots, aircraft mechanics, and aviation supply personnel responsible for the 120 planes initially assigned to the USS *Midway*.

Midway became a small town crammed inside a massive ship. Almost everything found ashore was part of *Midway*: a newspaper, radio station, library, laundry, jail, welding shops, repair shops, dry cleaning, chapel, power plant, barber shops, dentist's office, sewage plant, water plant, plumber's shop, hospital, gymnasium, ice-cream shops, pharmacy, convenience stores, and more. Each had to be operated by a group of sailors, many of them still teenagers.

Sailors sought entertainment whenever they could find it during long deployments and combat operations. Some bet on the exact time *Midway* would drop its anchor when it reached a foreign port.

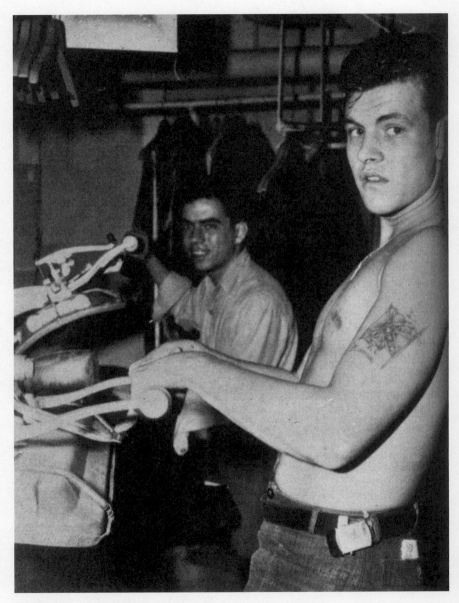

Midway was a floating city at sea with all types of jobs. Some sailors were assigned to the steam-filled laundry when they first reported aboard, prior to assignment to their permanent work station.

Midway's library contained 5,000 books.

Its population of 4,500 included young men from across America, many of whom had never seen the ocean. It also included hundreds of battle-scarred World War II veterans who had survived air-to-air dogfights high over the Pacific, sudden attacks by Japanese submarines, and even jumping into the sea as the ship under their feet sank to the bottom.

Midway stopped most sailors in their tracks the first time they walked up to the ship that soared more than 175 feet above them. The world had never seen such a large ship. It contained more than 2,500 miles of wiring connecting 12,000 lights and more than two

The huge size of the USS *Midway* amazed its crew. The four propellers each measured eighteen feet in diameter and weighed more than twenty tons. Each had to be perfectly balanced to operate properly for months at a time in the middle of the ocean.

thousand motors. More than three hundred heating and ventilation systems had been installed, along with firefighting sprinklers that sprayed 40,000 gallons of water a minute. At 968 feet, it was more than three football fields long, and its flight deck towered fifty feet above the ocean. Some of the 1,750 working and sleeping compartments were thirty feet below the waterline.

Officers handed each new sailor a booklet titled "This is the U.S.S. *Midway*, Largest, Fastest, Toughest Carrier Ever Built." It showed the crew how to tie socks together before sending them to the laundry. It reminded sailors: "When in doubt, 'SALUTE!'" They were told

Sailors spent thousands of hours cleaning, polishing, chipping, and painting *Midway*. A clean environment was more efficient, safe, and healthy. It extended the life of equipment but also came at a cost of tedious and boring-but-necessary work at sea.

Early crews aboard the USS *Midway* tested its unprecedented size and capability to determine how blimps, helicopters, and jets could operate on its flight deck. The carrier pioneered several naval aviation standards that later influenced Navy operations at sea.

"filthy language . . . stinks up the Navy just as much as it does at home" and encouraged everyone to buy National Service Insurance to protect their family in case they died in the line of duty. Officers taught sailors that they must always wear the proper uniform and never wear white socks with a uniform or sport beards or earrings.

Each sailor had to find his way through a maze of passageways and compartments to report to his department chief. The galleys' size overwhelmed John Rieman when he reported as a cook. *Midway* cooks prepared 13,500 meals every day. *Midway*'s coffeemakers

The galleys' best cooks were assigned to the eighty-gallon, steam-heated tubs where soups, sauces, and gravies were prepared. They had no temperature gauges so they could only judge when a batch was ready to be served by the sound of the steam.

brewed 10,000 cups at a time. Bakers baked 1,000 loaves of bread every night. Two barrels of flour were required to fill a single dough mixer. If potatoes were on the menu, 3,000 pounds had to be peeled the night before. If the menu included beef, butchers had to trim and prepare 4,250 pounds of it. Every recipe was written in increments of 100 servings.

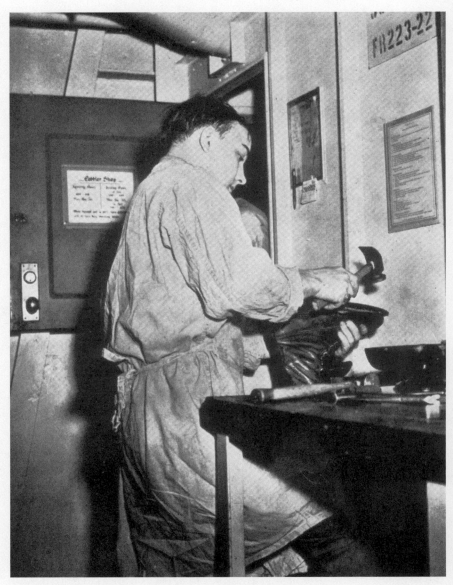

As a floating city at sea, *Midway* required a wide range of skills within its crew, from shoe repair to carpentry. Oftentimes, a skill that a sailor developed in the Navy became the basis for his career when he returned to civilian life.

Midway remained a warship, even though it joined the U.S. Navy fleet eight days after the end of World War II. In late 1945, Francis Derby and the rest of the crew sailed for the Caribbean aboard *Midway* to test its design, construction, and fighting capability. Derby had enlisted at age seventeen to avoid the draft. The Worcester, New York, native was a carpenter on *Midway*, an all-steel ship. Other than repairing cabinets and furniture in officers' staterooms and offices, he had little to do. One day during a seagoing test, he nearly dropped his saw when *Midway*'s engines suddenly were thrown into reverse while steaming at full speed. The captain needed to know if the carrier could handle a sudden stop at that speed. A fierce shudder ran down the ship's spine and up the legs of Derby and every sailor on *Midway*. The carrier held together as the massive propellers reversed their spin.

The crew discovered that *Midway*'s designers had placed a low priority on their comfort. Although *Midway* had 291 blowers that

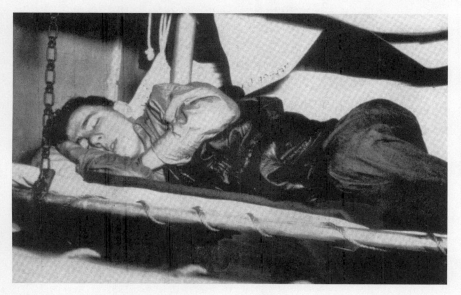

Sailors slept in canvas bunks stacked three high. On cruises to the tropics, a lack of air conditioning led to hot, humid sleeping compartments and sometimes moldy bunks. More than one hundred sailors slept in a single compartment.

pushed air through six miles of vents, the floating steel honeycomb absorbed and retained heat. The heat and humidity inside the ship became unbearable when *Midway* arrived in the Caribbean. Mildew began to grow on the sailors' canvas bunks. For some it got so bad that they dragged their thin mattresses to a secluded spot outside and slept under the stars.

In some compartments, crew bunks were stacked four high. The top bunk was so close to the ceiling, called the bulkhead on a ship, that a man couldn't turn over in his bed. To roll over, he had to climb down onto the deck, turn around, and then climb up over three sleeping sailors back into his bunk. It nearly caused a mutiny on *Midway*. When the carrier returned to port, many bunks were relocated so they could be three high instead of four.

The 400 officers on *Midway* slept in groups of 2 to 8, depending on their rank. Only the captain, his executive officer, and the admiral (who was responsible for the ships that sailed with and protected *Midway*) enjoyed traditional, freestanding beds in private bedrooms. Most sailors on the carrier slept in large compartments that held more than one hundred bunks. The aisles between them were only about two feet wide. A sailor couldn't pass another without turning sideways. The youngest and newest sailors were forced to sleep in bunks almost on the floor at the entrance. They rarely slept more than an hour at a time without someone walking by them. Privacy became a distant memory on *Midway*.

Sailors also were assigned bunks closest to their duty stations. The forty corpsmen slept in a room next to the sick bay. Many of the 200 cooks slept in a single compartment one level below the main galley in the middle of the ship. Usually only one or two ladders (among hundreds on *Midway*) separated crammed living quarters from where sailors worked. A sailor might spend eighteen months on the carrier and see less than 20 percent of the ship. Sailors were discouraged from wandering through engineering plants, welding shops, or aircraft engine repair compartments. If a sailor didn't have business there, he had no business being there.

As a result, the USS *Midway* was composed of dozens of neighborhoods. A sailor slept, ate, worked, and played games with buddies in his medical, supply, aircraft repair, engineering, flight-deck, security, or other department. His loyalty started with the man next to him and extended perhaps to the chief petty officer who commanded him.

Sailors lived only a few feet from their work stations. These men, responsible for *Midway*'s massive anchor chains, slept just below the flight deck, where the aircraft were launched.

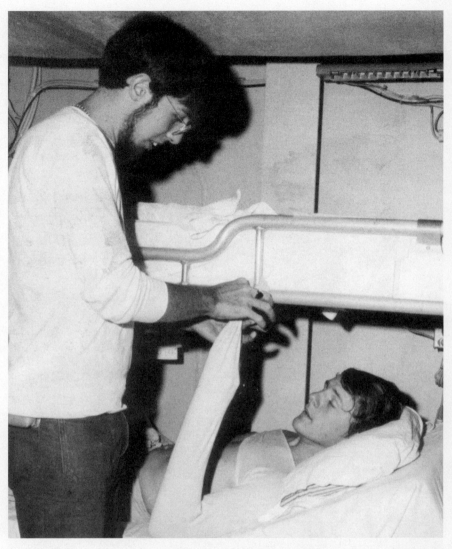

Comprehensive medical facilities were aboard *Midway*, including a hospital, called "sick bay," that included an intensive-care unit, two operating rooms, X-ray facilities, exam rooms, and a pharmacy. Only the sickest and most badly injured sailors were assigned to beds in sick bay. Next door was the dentist's office.

Usually the chief was a "grizzled veteran" in his early thirties. Young sailors learned to share their problems with their chief. In turn, he taught them how to cope in a life dictated every waking moment by the orders of others. He also taught them how to sober up after the last night on liberty, how to take care of a new tattoo, how easily a descending elevator could decapitate a careless sailor, or how a band saw could cut a hand in two if he didn't pay attention. Chiefs turned teenagers from Denver, San Diego, Waco, and Columbus into men. Chiefs ran the Navy, teaching and training one sailor at a time.

Midway's captain commanded all the neighborhoods aboard the carrier. In many ways he acted as the mayor of a floating city at sea. It was his job to get the neighborhoods to work together for months at a time, sometimes in the most brutal conditions possible. Twice as old as most of his crew, the captain strove to inspire green sailors. There was "the Navy way, the right way, and then there's the *Midway*," and he trusted his department heads to teach that. It was vital on *Midway*'s first mission.

America's relations with the Soviet Union's leader, Joseph Stalin, had become extremely strained in 1946. Stalin wanted to establish communism across Eastern Europe, while Pres. Harry Truman viewed expanding Soviet influence as a threat to democratic European countries. It became known as the Cold War: a battle of threats, moves, feints, and nerves between the United States and Soviet Union over world influence that stopped just short of open warfare.

The Soviet sub-Arctic worried American military planners. The Soviet Union had massive naval bases near the Arctic Circle, not far from Finland and Norway. The Soviets had the ability to invade Western Europe from the frozen north. The U.S. Navy had fought World War II mostly in the warm waters of the Pacific Ocean. Could the Navy stop a Soviet invasion in freezing conditions?

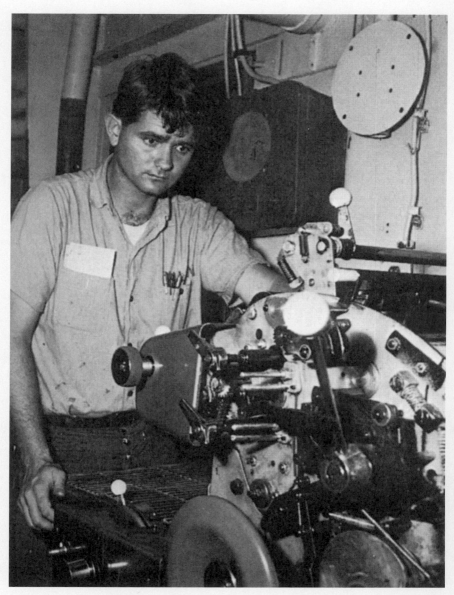

The majority of *Midway* sailors spent only a few years in the Navy, many of them learning skills that they used to build careers as civilians. As a floating city at sea, *Midway* produced pressmen, journalists, electricians, mechanics, nurses, X-ray technicians, pilots, tailors, policemen, attorneys, and others.

In a floating city at sea, there was no landfill for garbage. Classified documents were burned, while the bulk of refuse generated by 4,500 men went over the side of the ship.

The USS *Midway* would find out. In March 1946, Capt. A. K. Morehouse was in command when the aircraft carrier pulled out of Norfolk, turned north, and steamed toward Greenland—and weather that threatened to freeze a man's tear ducts shut forever if he didn't stay focused and remember his training.

Only six months old, *Midway* became the first carrier to operate extensively that far north in the winter. The sailors would have to find ways to keep aircraft in flying condition as sleet and snow blew across *Midway*'s slick, ice-covered flight deck.

Ten days after the ship left port, the weather roughened, the wind stiffened to thirty-five miles an hour, and *Midway*'s anti-aircraft guns next to Donald Fry crusted with ice. He had dropped out of high school as a junior in April 1945 and enlisted in the Navy. The bitter cold on *Midway* reminded him of winter storms in his hometown of York, Pennsylvania.

Waves approaching from the side threatened to sweep Fry, Buddy Herrmann, Tom Turner, and Don Struchen out of their gun turrets and into the sea. When the weather calmed slightly, they practiced firing the guns at targets pulled by aircraft. *Midway* had more guns than any of the forty aircraft carriers that had been built previously. Their job was to defend *Midway* in the last seconds when enemy aircraft descended to attack the ship. Within a few years, however, the arrival of powerful, high-altitude jets would render a carrier's anti-aircraft guns ineffective.

Then matters got worse as huge waves hit *Midway* head on. Usually fifty feet above the water, *Midway*'s bow dug into the waves, sending green, roiling water racing down the flight deck toward the stern. Because the carrier was so large, pilots who approached from the rear to land said when the bow dug into a wave, they could see the deck bend at the middle flight-deck expansion joint. The joints allowed the flight deck to bend in heavy seas but also allowed water into the ship's interior. Sailors who worked directly under the flight deck sometimes were soaked by torrents of water that cascaded through the expansion joints.

In heavy seas, aircraft could slide off the flight deck if they were not properly secured. Each aircraft's "plane crew" was responsible for its safety. They used heavy chains to secure the planes to the flight deck.

Sub-Arctic storms relentlessly assaulted *Midway*. When Fry was off duty and in his bunk three levels below the flight deck, he saw water running down *inside* the aircraft carrier's hull. When seas stayed rough, the cooks on *Midway* stopped cooking for fear of burning themselves. The aircraft carrier's galleys contained steam kettles, deep-fat fryers, and griddles the size of picnic tables. In rough seas, the most the sailors could expect from John Rieman and the rest of the cooks was coffee and sandwiches.

When *Midway* changed direction during this particular storm, the carrier started rolling from side to side. Joe Delaney's eyes widened

The USS *Midway* was built on what originally was a battleship-hull design. That made it very top heavy and prone to extreme rolling in high seas. New sailors often experienced seasickness only a few hours after leaving port for the first time. Some sailors called *Midway* the "USS *Rock 'n' Roll.*"

with each roll from one wave's crest to the next. *Midway* had been built on a hull concept originally contemplated for a lighter battleship. The narrow hull with a wide steel flight deck made *Midway* extremely top heavy. Back and forth the carrier rolled as sailors deep inside *Midway* grew green with seasickness.

Many young men aboard *Midway* were seeing the ocean for the first time. Few knew if they were prone to seasickness. Diesel fumes, greasy fried food, and claustrophobia made some sick before the ship left the pier. Some had to carry a bucket. When they felt nausea coming on, they stopped, threw up into the bucket, and then went back to work. Usually a sailor got over his seasickness after a week of very little food, vomiting, and dry heaves. For many, the sub-Arctic deployment brought a fresh round of illness.

Even if he were seasick, a sailor was expected to report for duty every day. When at sea, sailors worked seven days a week and looked forward to liberty ashore when *Midway* pulled into a foreign port.

It was even worse for *Midway* sailors ordered to stand out in the howling wind for hours at a time. Those who stood "smoke watch" had the coldest and most dangerous job. Perched on the highest platform on the mast, they reported whenever they saw the smoke rising from *Midway*'s twelve smokestacks darken. That indicated the fuel mixture needed adjustment. The ship's doctors discovered that the lookout's body temperature dropped four degrees during a four-hour watch in brutal wind and cold weather. Orders were issued that limited duty outside to two hours.

Meanwhile on the flight deck, Bill Larkin leaned into the gale. Before being assigned to *Midway*, he had patrolled the East Coast during World War II. Once, as his transport headed south to Puerto Rico, he saw a tanker torpedoed off the Georgia coast by a German submarine. On *Midway* he was a plane captain, making sure the planes were ready before the pilots climbed in. He needed three pairs of gloves to keep his fingers from freezing as snow whipped across the pitching deck. Larkin and others wrapped special blankets around aircraft engines to warm the motor oil. Sometimes they built small campfires under the engines to keep the oil from freezing, using their bodies as a windbreak. Larkin had one of the most dangerous jobs on *Midway*.

Aircraft crew chiefs such as Ray Shirley faced their own challenges. A pitching, windy, and snow-covered flight deck made it difficult to carry bombs to planes and attach them to wings and fuselages. There was no rail at the edge of the flight deck to keep Shirley from falling or being blown over the side and into the sea.

The ingenuity and dedication of Larkin and the flight-deck crew triumphed over weeks of bitter cold off the coast of Greenland.

Midway's pilots faced unique dangers of their own. If one crashed, near-freezing water became his enemy and life was measured in minutes. Pilots received specific instructions on how to wear the new rubberized nylon "poopy suit" they had been issued: wear long underwear, two pairs of socks, two pairs of gloves, and a scarf. Avoid overheating and sweating by dressing slowly. Take your time, because perspiration becomes ice in the sub-Arctic. Walk to the plane. And don't touch freezing metal with bare hands.

Pilots learned they had to put the poopy suit on correctly if they hoped to survive a crash in frigid water. If one failed to tie the trouser bottoms tightly or neglected to cinch the scarf around his neck, thirty-five-degree water seeped inside the suit. A leaking suit would fill with seawater and pull him under the surface before a destroyer or helicopter could rescue him.

Early pilot rescues were as dangerous as plane crashes. This pilot was accidentally dropped on *Midway*'s flight deck when a rescue helicopter had difficulty landing.

The USS *Midway* returned to Norfolk, Virginia after a deployment to the Mediterranean in 1951. Note the single "straight deck" and the anti-aircraft guns on the bow. The carrier's angle deck was added in 1955-57.

On March 26, 1946, *Midway* turned south and left the Labrador Sea, reaching New York City on March 28. The crew had set several new winter-operations standards in naval aviation. Its pilots had crashed into paralyzing waters, and all but one had survived. Flight-deck crews had learned how to launch and recover planes in weather that froze flesh and water in minutes. A green, largely untested crew had developed a sense of unity from having overcome unimaginable danger. *Midway*'s pioneers came home armed with self-confidence and pride. They had blazed a new naval aviation trail among the icebergs. The Navy better understood how to fly in severe weather.

For a few sailors, it marked the beginning of a Navy career. Most, however, left the Navy in two or four years, embarking on a civilian life far afield from their Navy training. Ray Shirley fired guns in the Navy but became a communications professor at the University of Tennessee. Buddy Herrmann left *Midway*'s gun turrets to work for a Texas utility company for forty-three years. Don Struchen also left *Midway*'s anti-aircraft gun turrets to work for a propane gas company in Iowa. After four years in the Navy, John Rieman left the Navy went on to get his high-school degree and then worked in a Boston machine shop for the next thirty-six years. Navy carpenter Francis Derby left the Navy after ten years and spent the rest of his life repairing and refinishing furniture. Tom Turner ultimately served more than thirty-one years in the Marine Corps and fought in the Korean War and in Vietnam.

The beginning of *Midway*'s odyssey also marked the beginning of many young men's adult lives.

Chapter 2

Naval Pioneers

In 1947, America feared a new enemy. An uneasy alliance with the Soviet Union's general secretary, Joseph Stalin, during World War II had dissolved into bitter mistrust and conflicting world objectives. Europe had once again become a battlefield of sorts. This time the United States and the Soviet Union dueled for influence over the countries that had been destroyed in or created during the war. One saw rebuilding as an opportunity for democracy; the other envisioned communism sweeping across World War II's ruins.

America had paid dearly in World War II and was now stripped of manpower and resources. Nearly three hundred thousand Americans had been killed, and the war had cost $288 million. Now it was time for the survivors to come home and rebuild their lives. Many had been away at war for four years and still were in their early twenties.

Those who remained in uniform faced a new world order. They would be expected to make sense of nuclear weapons and "serve" in the Cold War between the United States and the Soviet Union. They would be confronted by new technology that would lead to missile warfare and dramatic advances in jet aircraft. Some would make major contributions aboard the USS Midway.

No sailor in the Navy stood as proud as Tom Murphy on July 4, 1947, when he reported for duty aboard the USS *Midway*. The Indiana native was actually a member of the U.S. Marine Corps.

Midway always had a group of about seventy Marines, who provided the security aboard the carrier.

Murphy had enlisted a year earlier when he feared he might lose his job in the local ice plant for the winter. When his mother pointed out a newspaper article that reported the GI Bill was about to expire, Murphy decided to enlist to qualify for its veterans' college benefits. A brother and two cousins had served in the Navy. He could join that branch for four years or the Marines for only two. The teenager who loved to play basketball chose the Marines. After he completed sea school, orders came to report to the USS *Midway*.

A few weeks later, a train engine pulling three nondescript boxcars across Chesapeake Bay arrived on the pier alongside the USS *Midway*. Each held a rocket nestled in a cradle, ready to be hoisted aboard. When sailors eased them out into the morning sun, the mysterious cargo's secret was revealed: *German V-2 Rocket, U.S. Army Ordnance Dept. White Sand Proving Grounds, New Mex.* was painted in simple block letters on each side.

In the final days of World War II, American soldiers had discovered Adolf Hitler's massive rocket plant buried inside a German mountain. It took more than 350 railroad cars to move the rockets and their equipment to American ships for transport to the United States. A testing program began almost immediately. Officials wondered whether an aircraft carrier could survive the launch of a V-2 rocket from its flight deck. (All the V-2 rockets in World War II had taken off from the ground.) The USS *Midway* crew would determine if a ship could withstand a rocket launch. Tom Murphy and other Marines guarded the rockets on *Midway*'s hangar deck when the ship headed for Bermuda on September 2, 1947, on Operation Sandy.

Soon the carrier and crew fell into the natural rhythm of sailing in blue water. When Bermuda's pink beaches came into sight, *Midway* had arrived in some of the calmest water found anywhere in the

Officers marveled at a secret German V-2 rocket brought aboard the USS *Midway* for a daring launch from the flight deck. No one knew if ships could withstand the thrust of rocket launches.

Atlantic. The few sailors who had a job during the rocket launch took their positions. Neal Casey had escaped Oklahoma by joining the Navy the year before. He was assigned to "Sky One" to track the V-2 and call its range down to *Midway*'s plotting room. Gerald Bazinet, a graduate of a Catholic high school in the Bronx, was a fierce anticommunist. He had enlisted upon graduation and was assigned to a firefighting squad. He donned his fire suit and took his position at the edge of the flight deck.

Others, such as Murphy, sneaked out onto the catwalk along the edge of the flight deck, hoping to watch the historic launch. Most, though, were below deck. Ray Dall and others paced back and forth, looking up at the bulkhead as if they might see through it to the flight deck and spot the upright rocket at the stern. A huge iron ball full of liquid fuel sat not far away.

When a civilian scientist hit the launch button, the metal frame supporting the rocket shuddered as a deep growl erupted from the base of the V-2. A rumble spread through the ship, along the bulkheads, and into everyone aboard. A whitish orange flame flared sideways from between the rocket's fins. The V-2 wobbled for a moment, as if trying to make up its mind whether to leave *Midway*. Grayish-black smoke billowed up both sides of the rocket as it inched upward into the sky—then things went wrong.

The V-2 rose slightly and then leaned almost over on its side. Spotter Casey tracked the rocket as it headed for the carrier's island instead of rising high into the sky. It missed by only about one hundred yards. Right after it passed Casey's post, the V-2 veered toward the USS *Knox* steaming alongside *Midway*. At that point, scientists blew up the rocket. Its flight had lasted only twelve seconds, and it had risen about five thousand feet.

Several weeks later, the crew was surprised to hear the federal government claim that the wobbling rocket test had been a success. Despite the V-2's scary trajectory off the deck of *Midway*, the carrier had survived. Properly fortified warships could withstand the thrust of missiles. Now missile warfare could be combined with aircraft-carrier flight operations. Tom Murphy, Neal Casey, and thousands of other sailors had stood at the dawn of naval missile warfare aboard the USS *Midway*.

Midway's accomplishment came in a world of increasing uncertainty. Six months earlier, Pres. Harry Truman established the "Truman Doctrine," which promised American support for countries that resisted the spread of communism. Tension ruled the world. The Soviet Union sent twelve army divisions to its Turkish border, threatening invasion. Ethnic violence raged in Yugoslavia. The communist party grew stronger in war-ravaged Italy. Then England stunned the world when it announced it no longer could afford sending foreign aid to Turkey and Greece. The Eastern Mediterranean threatened to explode.

The V-2 rocket nearly hit *Midway*'s island. Scientists in charge of the experiment blew up the rocket before it reached the USS *Knox* about a mile away. *Midway* survived the launch in what became known as the dawn of naval missile warfare.

The USS *Midway*, America's largest and most powerful ship, sailed into the Mediterranean in November 1947 on the first of several deployments there. Sailing at the "Tip of the Atlantic Fleet's Sword," *Midway* stood ready to respond within hours if civil unrest in Italy, Greece, or Turkey threatened to boil over into war. *Midway* would ensure that American interests were protected by keeping the Suez Canal open. Some *Midway* sailors would bear more than their share of that responsibility.

John Pruitt, a nearly illiterate Texas runaway with an accent as thick as a stand of ironwood, always had the toughest work assignments aboard *Midway*. He sent most of his Navy pay to his divorced mother, two brothers, and a sister after ironing buddies' clothes, sewing buttons, and standing others' watches to make extra money. He didn't know John Mee. Only nineteen, Mee had already served three

Midway completed a series of deployments to the Mediterranean in all types of weather. These aircraft, with wings folded to save space, are crusted with snow and ice. In the years following World War II, civil unrest made the Mediterranean a very dangerous region.

years in the Navy after leaving the family dairy farm in New York and enlisting by lying about his age. He survived Japanese kamikaze attacks against the USS *Intrepid* in World War II. Amazingly, six of his brothers and sisters had served in the military as well.

On February 11, 1948, the USS *Midway* was anchored off Gulf D'Hyers, France. Hundreds of *Midway* sailors took small boats called launches to shore in rotating liberty shifts. John Pruitt was one. When it was time for him to return to the carrier, a fierce wind filled the Mediterranean with whitecaps. Rolling waves plowed into the launches crammed with sailors due back on *Midway*. A thundering wave hit Pruitt's launch hard, filling it waist-high with water. Some men tried to bail the water out with their hands, while others froze in terror. The launch had no chance when the second wave hit it—it swept Pruitt and dozens of sailors into the sea.

Pruitt tried to stay with the overturned launch as his waterlogged pea coat pulled him down. He took it off, along with his pants. Pruitt weakened quickly in the cold winter water. As the waves rolled over him, he couldn't tell which way was up to the surface. Only the roiled phosphorous that made an eerie film of light at the surface showed Pruitt where to find air.

An hour later, the blowing ocean stung John Mee's eyes as he stood at the bow of a search boat. His launch climbed over wave crests and crashed into the troughs as he searched for hours. He peered into the wet night for signs of life in the froth. Every once in a while, "Ho!" rang out over the waves' roar if a lookout spotted a floating body. Sometimes it was alive. Mee and others pulled *Midway* survivors out of the sea all night long, including John Pruitt.

Wearing only his undershorts and one sock, Pruitt ached from constant shivering. By the next morning, John Mee and the other rescuers also had collected eight men who had drowned. The tragedy became the single largest loss of life in *Midway*'s history up to that point. But it could have been worse. John Mee had helped pull twenty-nine exhausted men into wooden boats in the middle of a Mediterranean winter storm.

The USS *Midway* continued patrolling throughout the Mediterranean in the late 1940s, as the Cold War between the United States and the Soviet Union intensified. One patrol came during a spike in world turmoil and uncertainty. For nearly a year, the Soviets prevented civilian supplies from reaching West Berlin, an isolated noncommunist city in the middle of communist East Germany. The Soviets then shocked the world by detonating their first nuclear bomb. Partly in response, America and its allies formed the North Atlantic Treaty Organization (NATO) in 1949 to defend Europe against

When a sailor died in a shipboard accident, a burial service at sea was held. Only his personal belongings were sent home to a grieving family that would never see him again.

a possible Soviet invasion. To the east, Mao Tse Tung formally pro-claimed the communist People's Republic of China. Uncertainty gripped a nervous crew as *Midway* patrolled the Mediterranean.

The crew sailed on America's first carrier large enough to carry nuclear weapons. Some of America's earliest nuclear weapons were assigned to *Midway*. Although planes carrying nuclear bombs took

Emergency crews trained constantly aboard *Midway*. Plane crashes, fires, weapon malfunctions, and hazardous materials all made life aboard an aircraft carrier potentially dangerous.

off from the carrier, it lacked the capability for them to land. If a strike order had been issued, *Midway*'s pilots would fly to their targets, drop their nuclear payloads, and then try to outfly the nuclear blast toward a friendly landing strip. *Midway*'s pilots knew that nuclear strikes would be a one-way trip.

Sailors such as Bob Kennedy feared nuclear attacks. Kennedy came from a poor railroad family in Brainerd, Minnesota. Once when he came home from boot camp to visit, the family thought it would be fun not to tell Kennedy that they had moved before their house was demolished. The Kennedy family loved to play practical jokes. Things were serious on *Midway*, where Kennedy and the crew trained for a possible nuclear attack at sea. It was called "ABC Warfare" (atomic, biological, and chemical attacks). They learned that a nuclear bomb detonated underwater sends a shock wave through the steel decks of ships at sea, breaking sailors' legs and backs. A bomb exploding on the surface produces a fireball exceeding one million degrees Centigrade.

Mustard gas was another worry. If the enemy fired missiles filled with mustard gas at *Midway*, the crew could not possibly abandon ship in time. In the event of an attack, Kennedy and the others had to get inside the ship as fast as possible and close every opening to the outside world. Each hatch and fitting had a sailor responsible for its immediate closure. *Midway* even had mustard-gas-sensitive crayons, whose marks on metal turned bright blue if exposed to mustard gas.

Japanese kamikaze attacks on wooden aircraft-carrier decks during World War II only five years earlier had already become ancient history. Instead, *Midway*'s crew trained to guard, assemble, load, and launch nuclear weapons. They practiced defending themselves against fireballs and caustic gasses. Yet a primal nautical fear dating back to the earliest wooden ships remained undiminished: fire at sea.

Bob Kennedy tended a storeroom "so far down in the ship I heard the water rushing along the ship's hull at night." One day, an officer sent him to deliver an aircraft part "on the double." His mission completed, Kennedy decided to take a break for dinner and then watch a movie before returning to his storeroom and making sure everything was in order.

"Fire, Storeroom Charlie 530 Able."

Kennedy's blood ran cold when he heard the booming public-address announcement. He pictured a trashcan full of uncovered, oily, combustible rags in his storeroom and panicked. He ran to the fantail, fearing an explosion. Meanwhile, fire crews in the ship's damage-control division raced to Kennedy's storeroom and doused a smoldering can. Someone had probably dropped a cigarette through the grating from the deck above.

The next day—after a sleepless night—Kennedy stood ramrod straight in front of Capt. W. M. Beakley. The justice system aboard

In an emergency, nearly every sailor was assigned to a specific location with specific emergency duties. Officers emphasized the need for sailors to report to their emergency stations and wait for orders.

Midway was as swift as it was straightforward. The ship's captain acted as judge and jury. The crew included a prosecutor who presented charges as well as legal officers who defended the accused. The captain had the authority to impose immediate penalties for lesser offenses or proceed with a more formal court-martial for more serious crimes. Potential penalties ranged from extra work assignments to demotion in rank, the loss of liberty ashore, a jail sentence, or even the death penalty in the most extreme cases.

Kennedy knew that Beakley could send him straight to a jail cell in the brig. Just below the ship's largest galley, the brig had four barred cells guarded night and day by Marines such as Braden Kruger. He had joined the Marines to avoid being drafted by the Army. Tall and thin, Kruger had pretty much been on his own since his father left the family when Kruger was twelve years old. Some of the prisoners in the cells he guarded were from other ships because they had committed serious crimes, ranging from assault to theft. With no air conditioning, the steel cells cooked in the summertime heat. When the brig's inmates were escorted to the second-deck galley to eat, other sailors turned their backs on them.

Kennedy knew committing a crime violated the crew's trust. Nothing was more sacred at sea than trust. Witnesses confirmed that Kennedy had been ordered to deliver a part and was late returning to his work station. Captain Beakley's piercing eyes sized up the youngster before imposing fifteen days' restriction. That meant two weeks of extra, backbreaking work details. Kennedy and his buddies in aviation supply never left flammable material unattended again.

Midway's crew of 4,500 young men represented a cross-section of America. There were achievers, leaders, followers, and loafers. Some were loud, others were quiet, and a few were loners. Some were confident while others were unsure and even fearful. A handful liked to cut corners and a few were criminals. They were all young and liked to have a good time.

The Marines aboard the USS *Midway* were its police force. They provided security for the captain, guarded missiles and secret compartments, and ran the jail deep inside the aircraft carrier.

330

The *Midway* crew was a microcosm of America. Ethnic tensions occasionally surfaced, just as they did ashore as the nation grappled with various race issues. Sometimes conflicts were made worse by extremely crowded conditions at sea.

Rows of stacked aircraft batteries made the air thick and acrid in the small battery locker. The room had only two entrances, one from an interior passageway and another from the sponson deck. It was the perfect place to run illegal craps games each payday.

Sailors were paid every two weeks, collecting between $83.20 and $99.37 each payday. Some went to *Midway*'s post office and sent money home to families desperate for it. A sailor did not need much money on the ship. He could buy razors, cigarettes, snacks, and ice cream. Or he could gamble. Hundreds of *Midway* sailors gambled. Most played poker (draw and seven-card stud) or craps. A few sailors were loan sharks, offering loans to gamblers on a run of bad luck or sailors who needed money before going ashore on liberty.

On the night of March 15, 1952, Bill Grabowski sensed a killing was about to be made. A Connecticut high-school dropout, Grabowski had enlisted with some buddies two years earlier. He left a large Polish family headed by a hardworking, illiterate father who worked in a mill to feed six children. Grabowski was tall, lanky, and likeable. Very outgoing, he enjoyed bragging about his girlfriends and played craps.

Late that night, twenty sailors who had been winners earlier in the day crowded around the homemade craps table. A single light bulb swung back and forth overhead. Suddenly, three bandits entered the locker with pistols. Each wore his hat inside out and pulled down low over his eyes, almost to the neckerchief covering his face. Long-sleeved pea coats covered them from chin to foot. All wore gloves to hide rings and tattoos. They grabbed the money off the table and ordered the gamblers to empty their pockets. In minutes the robbers were gone, closing the hatches to the locker as they left.

Grabowski and the others were not about to chase the armed robbers but they had an idea. They raced back to their sleeping compartments to see if anyone appeared out of breath, as if he had just returned on the run. No luck—they never saw their money again.

The next week, newspapers around the world carried reports of the craps-game robbery. More than four thousand dollars was taken, enough to buy a Jaguar X120 or make a large down payment on a house in 1952. A lengthy investigation followed, in part led by Capt. Wendell Morrisset, who was in charge of Marines aboard *Midway*. The Marines guarded the captain and the admiral when he was aboard. They also were responsible for guarding *Midway*'s nuclear bombs.

Morrisset went "by the book" more than most *Midway* sailors. His eyes burned with determination. The native of Lubbock, Texas, had enlisted during World War II as soon as he turned seventeen years old. A long, straight nose sat between a square jaw and a receding hairline. He kept an organizational table that reassigned part of the ship's crew to become an amphibious landing force in case of a sudden invasion. As it became apparent that the robbers had escaped, Morrisset did not know that the military was discussing two possible emergency deployments of his Marines and perhaps part of *Midway*'s crew. One was against the Soviet Union and the other against China.

The Kola Peninsula's birch forest shuddered as thousands of Soviet soldiers crossed nearly frozen marshes in September 1952. Dockworkers loaded bombs and supplies onto Soviet warships in Murmansk, only 100 miles from the Norwegian border. The Soviets were mobilizing. Were they about to invade Europe?

Half a world away, communist party chairman Mao Tse Tung strengthened his grip on the three-year-old People's Republic of China. He had pushed nationalist Gen. Chiang Kai-shek and his troops off the mainland onto the island of Formosa and nearby coastal islands. Most of the islands were within range of mainland artillery. Chiang Kai-shek called for an American invasion of China to help him reclaim it from the communists.

One threat was real, the other imaginary. While Chinese tensions increased, the Soviet mobilization toward Norway existed only in the imagination of American military planners. It became the basis of a massive international sea exercise in the North Atlantic called Operation Mainbrace. *Midway* played a key role among the 160 ships from eight NATO countries. More than eighty thousand sailors participated in amphibious landings and air operations under brutal conditions. Meanwhile, Soviet spy ships disguised as fishing trawlers sailed on the horizon, watching the exercises and reporting new ocean battle tactics to headquarters.

They observed men such as Jim Gorman, who fueled planes on the flight deck and bore the brunt of wicked weather. Unending winds cut through every man and threatened frostbite. Gloves and shoes had no extra lining. Day after day, Gorman found ways to stand upright in a cold hurricane wind without getting blown overboard north of the Arctic Circle. Operating under "battle conditions" as the icy flight deck rolled back and forth in the relentless waves, a man could only hope for a sandwich and cup of coffee to warm his insides. By the time the exercise had ended, several *Midway* sailors suffered frostbite and frozen ears and tear ducts.

In addition to exercises involving dozens of ships, some training on *Midway* in the early 1950s was secret. As the Soviet Union strengthened its grip on Eastern Europe, many Americans feared that another war in Europe might include the use of nuclear weapons. The Soviets were developing thermonuclear bombs. Meanwhile, the USS *Midway* patrolled the Mediterranean in late 1952 with closely guarded Mk-7 nuclear bombs.

As Christmas 1952 approached, the U.S. nuclear-bomb arsenal totaled 850. Several were aboard *Midway*. On Christmas Eve, *Midway* anchored near Cannes, France. A cold wind kept most of the crew aboard. Shortly after midnight, pilots and plane crews from two squadrons gathered around the Christmas tree on the hangar deck. Marines guarded closed hatches and secured the hangar deck's fire doors to ensure a silent night.

On each side of the Christmas tree, an attack aircraft had been parked. Next to the tree were two nuclear bombs, each about ten feet long. They were four times more powerful than the bombs dropped on Hiroshima and Nagasaki that had ended World War II. While nearly the entire *Midway* crew slept in the early hours of Christmas Day, a handful of men practiced loading and unloading nuclear weapons inside the silent ship.

One young sailor sleeping several decks below was John Clancy. A year earlier he and his brother had walked across New York's Times Square to buy clothes. They watched an antiwar movie called *Steel Helmet*. It somehow inspired Clancy to drop out of high school and enlist in the Navy as soon as he turned eighteen. Loose and gangly, he kept his red hair long so that it fell down onto his forehead. His wide eyes often were serious. He was the oldest of eight children.

Not far from Clancy, a sailor a few years older slept soundly. John Hipp had graduated from the Naval Academy and had a bright future. It was Hipp's job to train Clancy and build others into an efficient team in his division. He took a personal interest in each man who worked for him on *Midway*.

Sailors deep inside *Midway* had to be retrained on operating vital equipment each time the aircraft carrier completed a major modernization project that added new technology.

Practice drills were frequently held aboard *Midway*. Some sailors practiced taking large bombs, missiles, and rockets out of storage and attaching them to aircraft. Some bombs weighed 500 pounds.

Hipp had sensed that the young man from Far Rockaway, New York, needed help. So he took Clancy under his wing. One day Clancy watched another sailor fighting while on liberty ashore. Clancy lied to Captain Ashford so the sailor wouldn't get in trouble. Hipp saw right through Clancy. After the hearing, he took Clancy on a private walk across *Midway*'s flight deck. "That wasn't the right thing to do," said the junior officer, staring ahead off the bow. "I know why you did it, but it was wrong." Clancy stood silent. He knew where Hipp was headed. "That guy should have been punished for what he did. He'll always deserve what he gets. We all do, in the end. There's always accountability and responsibility."

When assigned to a department, sailors had to learn new skills and how to work with men they had never met. Sometimes they were assigned to shifts that required them to sleep during the day.

"Yeah," said Clancy as he stared at the deck, the wind whipping around him.

"The friends you choose will always reflect on you. You're better than you think you are," continued Hipp. "You just don't know it yet. So I'm going to show you. I'll tell you when you're square and doing it the right way. When you aren't, we'll talk about it privately. You're better than you think. Give yourself a chance to prove it."

Clancy, the high-school dropout, was touched. One day he decided to show his gratitude. He went to the gunnery maintenance shop and asked a sailor who moonlighted as a barber for a haircut, nice and short the way the Navy wanted. When Hipp saw Clancy the next day, the officer slapped Clancy on the back.

Chief petty officers, the most senior enlisted men on the ship, were responsible for training each newcomer on how to conduct himself as a sailor, as a member of the crew, and as an adult.

"You're going to make it, Red Dog," he said, hanging a nickname on Clancy that he proudly wore the rest of his life.

For nearly seven years *Midway* had patrolled the Mediterranean, giving political and ethnic enemies a moment of pause. Yet as the Mediterranean continued to simmer, a narrow sliver of ocean half a world away suddenly threatened to boil over. Two Chinas jockeyed for a potential showdown in 1954. The national Chinese leader on the island of Formosa, Chiang Kai-shek, had gathered 58,000 troops on Quemoy Island and another 15,000 on nearby Matsu, both only a few miles off the coast of communist mainland China. Day after day, Chairman Mao's artillery pounded the offshore islands.

In Washington, a major debate raged over whether or how the U.S. should get involved. On September 12, 1954, the Joint Chiefs of Staff recommended using nuclear weapons against communist China. Pres. Dwight Eisenhower, a hero as a World War II general, rejected the recommendation. Yet rumors echoed across the Norfolk, Virginia, waterfront, where the USS *Midway* rested after another Mediterranean mission.

"The U.S. is preparing for nuclear war!"

"The USS *Midway* will soon leave Norfolk and sail around the world for reassignment to the Pacific Fleet."

The second rumor proved true. *Midway* crossed the equator on January 6, 1955, as it sailed east toward the tip of Africa, the Indian Ocean, and the Western Pacific. When the crew woke up that morning, the huge aircraft carrier floated dead in the water. "Crossing the line" at the equator was a cherished Navy tradition. Sailors who had crossed the line before were called "shellbacks" and initiated the sailors who were crossing the line for the first time, known as "pollywogs." An entire day of pranks and practical jokes on *Midway*'s flight deck awaited the 2,850 pollywogs.

When *Midway* sailed into an international crisis, the captain depended on radar operators to watch for any potential threats, including unidentified aircraft flying toward the ship. They became the captain's eyes.

The flight deck had been converted into a torture zone. At one location, every pollywog had to kiss the naked, hairy belly of the fattest sailor on the ship—which was also covered with grease. Then another sailor slammed a fistful of flour in the pollywogs' greasy faces. Then it got worse. Some shellbacks sprayed pollywogs with a hose before they climbed into boxes the size of coffins that were filled with garbage. Then other shellbacks gave them haircuts with tin snips. The final test was exhausting and brutal: run the length of the flight deck between two lines of shellbacks who used planks to swat the bottoms, legs, and feet of pollywogs.

"For most of us, by the end of the day your butt was tore up and you were pretty black and blue," one sailor wrote home. "But when it was over, you felt a sense of relief you didn't know was possible. It was over. You made it through. You were a shellback. I never felt such an enormous sense of pride. We had unity. We were a team."

A few days later, *Midway* arrived at Capetown, South Africa. White and black *Midway* sailors had formed a unique bond from their common experience in the middle of the Atlantic Ocean. But they were prohibited from going ashore together in a city stained by apartheid.

For nine years, the USS *Midway* had patrolled a world that had lived in fear of a nuclear war erupting in Europe. Now *Midway* sailors prepared to sail into a new kind of war. It would be a war of constant and relentless threats, both real and imagined—the Cold War.

Chapter 3

Survivors at Sea

For more than two thousand years, most of the world's great wars had been fought throughout Europe and Asia Minor. Mesopotamian, Greek, Egyptian, and Roman empires had conquered and then collapsed. Seagoing imperialism by the British, Danish, Spanish, and others followed. Each dominated and then faded as the tides of world history flowed across the centuries.

By the middle of the twentieth century in the aftermath of World War II, world power once again had shifted. Two countries that centuries earlier had extended their influence far beyond their borders reemerged as dominant. Both were governed by communists: the Soviet Union and the People's Republic of China. Throughout the 1950s, the vast Pacific Ocean (65 million square miles) became a battlefield in an undeclared war as the Soviet Union's Navy expanded and China began exerting influence throughout Southeast Asia.

The United States' attention, and the USS Midway, *would be drawn into conflict and confrontation as a possible third world war loomed just over the horizon. The young Americans aboard* Midway *would repeatedly sail "at the tip of the sword" on an ocean of uncertainty.*

Heavy, ashen clouds blocked the sun on the morning of February 6, 1955. *Midway* was quiet. The crew had just completed its high-speed sprint across the Indian Ocean after receiving orders to join Task Force 77 off the coast of China. *Midway*'s sailors had been warned "this is the real deal."

Marty McCormick worked on the flight deck, preparing planes for launch. He had hated his job at the Philadelphia Electric Company after high school so he joined the Navy. When the ship's loudspeakers blared, "Flight quarters," he scrambled up a ladder near his bunk and jumped through an outside hatch at the edge of the flight deck. The sight on the horizon stopped him in his tracks.

He thought somehow he had been transported back to World War II. Aircraft carriers and their escorts sat on the horizon in every direction. Even a submarine surfaced for a few minutes to exchange signals with *Midway* and then submerged. This was no training drill, McCormick realized. The ammunition was live and it was combat conditions.

President Eisenhower had decided to evacuate the heavily populated Tachen Islands, including Quemoy and Matsu. More than thirty thousand nationalist soldiers and civilians had to be transported out of range of communist artillery on the mainland. Pilots from *Midway* and other carriers of Task Force 77 would fly air cover, silencing the artillery that had been blasting the islands.

More than most, McCormick knew how dangerous even routine flight operations could be. He and the others working the flight deck each had specific responsibilities and were trained to make instant decisions that could save lives. They communicated with hand signals on the windy, rolling flight deck. The crew reviewed emergency procedures as *Midway*'s aircraft began patrolling over Quemoy and Matsu. When one plane returned to the ship after a patrol and landed, a rocket somehow flew off the underside of the aircraft's wing, skidded down the flight deck, and wedged itself under another plane. McCormick dove onto the deck, "waiting for the fireball." Meanwhile, two young sailors responsible for aircraft ordnance ran out, pulled the rocket free, and threw it over the side before it could explode.

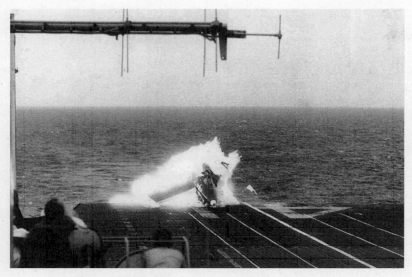

Everyone feared flight deck accidents. Here a pilot dropped too low on his approach, striking the stern and breaking his plane in half.

The plane rolled down the flight deck as a fireball fed by jet fuel mushroomed behind it.

Within seconds, trained fire crews braved the brutal heat and flames to put the fire out. Corpsmen raced to the cockpit. Amazingly, this pilot survived the crash, suffering only a broken leg.

"That was the last we saw of it, and it struck me how some kids, many twenty years old, acted with such bravery. Young guys like me had responsibilities that, if we were wrong in how we went about our business, people would die," said McCormick.

When the Navy's rescue boats, called LSTs, arrived alongside piers on the island, fleeing civilians brought everything they could carry and drag, including livestock. Hundreds of families crammed together on the main decks of the LSTs as *Midway* aircraft circled overhead. It was a rocky, dangerous way to escape the shelling on a path toward an unknown future. On one LST, a mountain of refugees' belongings shifted in the rough seas, crushing a child. The youngster was buried at sea. A small boy's flight to safety had been cruelly cut short and a homeless family devastated.

Within a few days, Task Force 77 completed its mission of evacuating thousands of Chinese off the Tachens. The USS *Midway* remained in the Western Pacific as reports of renewed tension between the Chinese factions grew even more alarming. Sec. of State John Foster Dulles publicly said the use of nuclear weapons was under consideration. President Eisenhower created a national uproar when he stated, "A-bombs can be used . . . as you would a bullet." The Chief of Naval Operations, Robert Carney, predicted war with China by mid-April. *Midway* stayed on station and its crew on alert. They wondered if they soon would launch aircraft to attack a new enemy.

Then China folded. On April 23, it announced a newfound willingness to negotiate with nationalist leaders on Formosa. About a week later, communist shelling of Quemoy and Matsu stopped. War had been averted for the time being. As *Midway* steamed toward Japan and then California, the communists continued their military buildup along the mainland coast. At the same time, the nationalists reinforced nearby islands with thousands of soldiers. Another Chinese crisis seemed inevitable. Perhaps *Midway* again would sail into seas of conflict that might erupt into war.

When the USS *Midway* passed under California's Golden Gate Bridge on July 14, 1955, it completed a 57,000-mile journey around the world. The crew had been at sea almost 190 days straight. The floating city at sea had consumed massive amounts of fuel, food, and other supplies. *Midway* had sailed at the end of a multi-thousand-mile relay race of supply ships that had arrived next to the carrier every three days. Some carried fuel; others arrived with food, X-ray film, engine parts, paper, ink, and everything else consumed by thousands of young men running a ship twenty-four hours a day for months at a time. Resupplying *Midway* was an extremely dangerous process called "underway replenishment," or UNREP for short. It was a nerve-wracking procedure that placed additional burdens on some *Midway* sailors.

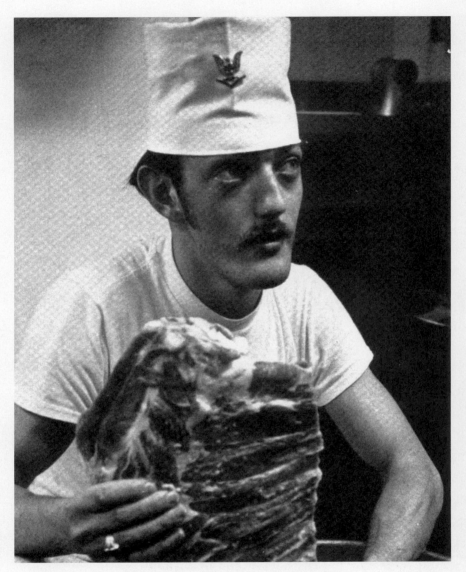

A crew of 4,500 consumed huge amounts of supplies. It required more than 4,000 pounds of meat just for one dinner. *Midway* cooks, bakers, and butchers prepared 13,500 meals every day.

   Helmsman Don Dresser was a tall, friendly youngster with an open face highlighted by bright blue eyes. When UNREP was under way, he held *Midway*'s broad steering wheel in his hands. *Midway* and the supply ship had to plow through the ocean, side by side, only 150 feet apart for hours at a time while supplies were transferred over to the carrier. If Dresser let *Midway* drift only one degree off course for a minute toward the right, the ship would move twenty feet and possibly collide with the supply ship. The dangers of UNREP sometimes were greater than combat.

   To relax, Dresser played basketball when the hangar deck was converted for recreation. Sometimes boxing tournaments as well as talent shows were held to boost ship's morale.

Occasionally the hangar deck was converted into volleyball courts, basketball courts, or boxing rings. Some events were competitive and sometimes they were entertaining. Sometimes boxers were blindfolded before entering the ring to swing away.

More than one hundred UNREPs had been completed by the time *Midway* arrived at a Seattle navy yard in late 1955. The carrier needed a massive overhaul. No crew would be needed during the modernization, so *Midway*'s sailors all received orders for new assignments.

Some left *Midway* quietly, while others slapped their buddies on the back on their way ashore. John Clancy, the New York high-school dropout, transferred to another ship. He walked slowly off *Midway* and paused on the pier, his sea bag against his leg. He turned and looked up at the carrier. There on the fantail stood John Hipp. Clancy thought about the hours they had spent together, talking about the future—laughing, revealing, teaching, and resolving. Clancy raised his hand to wave goodbye but stopped. A moment passed and then he snapped his best salute up at his friend John.

Midway's increased capacity after modernization would affect how often it had to be resupplied at sea. Oftentimes a Navy tanker (center) pumped fuel to *Midway* (right) and another Navy ship simultaneously.

Hipp did the same, his back straight, his eyes locked on Clancy. John Clancy had reached manhood on the USS *Midway*. Together, he and John Hipp had faced down the enemy. Both had been part of what had made the first decade of *Midway* magic.

Two years later, more than $55 million had been spent modernizing the USS *Midway*. More than 1.1 million days of labor had been spent by thousands of welders, sheet-metal workers, electricians, plumbers, machinists, and architects. As the USS *Midway* prepared to rejoin the U.S. Navy fleet in 1957, it bore little resemblance to what it looked like only two years earlier.

A second, short angled deck had been added to the side of the flight deck. For the first time, planes could land on this angled deck as other planes launched straight off the bow at the front of the ship. Simultaneous landings and takeoffs required a great deal of crew training on new equipment that had been installed. Some sailors would be trained to operate a new 50,000-pound crane. Others would learn how to operate the new steam-driven catapults that launched the aircraft. Their power could propel a seventeen-ton fighter jet from 0 to 150 miles an hour in only three seconds on the seventy-five-yard-long bow.

When *Midway* returned to sea for the first time, the crew tested every system on the huge aircraft carrier that now weighed 63,000 tons. That included 1,700 telephones, 2,000 electric motors, 14,000 lights, 600 loudspeakers, and 325 separate ventilation systems. They also checked more than 240 miles of electrical cables, 230 miles of tubing, four two-story turbines, and twelve boilers that created the steam for *Midway*'s power.

In addition, *Midway*'s fifty-three cooks and nineteen bakers tested new galley equipment to make sure they could prepare the 13,500 meals a day required to feed *Midway*'s crew. The supply division made sure there were enough ingredients available so bakers could bake 6,500 loaves of bread and others could churn 850 gallons of ice cream weekly.

Steam was the lifeblood of *Midway*. It fed the turbines that provided propulsion and powered the catapults for launching aircraft. Without steam, it was impossible for the carrier to go to sea, so its boilers were located in the most protected part of the ship.

As *Midway* demonstrated its operational readiness off the coast of California, rumblings of war between communist and nationalist China once again rolled in from the west. In 1957, the United States installed nuclear-capable missiles on Formosa that threatened mainland China. Talks between the U.S. and communist China broke down. Clearly, a larger U.S. Navy presence again would be required in the strait between Formosa and the mainland. The U.S. Navy turned to a war hero, Capt. John Thomas Blackburn, to become *Midway*'s next skipper. *Midway* sailors might need his daring if they returned to duty along the Chinese coast.

Some sailors, such as bakers, worked through the night so that *Midway* could operate twenty-four hours a day. Sailors worked seven days a week when at sea, including bakers who had to make nearly one thousand loaves of bread, plus pastries, cakes, and pies, almost every day.

Blackburn was a legendary character. He was short and heavy lidded and had a strong nose. The former combat pilot had shot down eleven Japanese fighters in World War II, more than ten years earlier. He was a hard-charging, hard-drinking commanding officer, and his bravado inspired tremendous loyalty. One day on *Midway*, he decided to fly an F-8 Crusader fighter jet, even though he had not been trained to fly the aircraft. Within minutes of takeoff, Blackburn lost control of the powerful fighter as it nearly dove into the ocean. He barely made it back aboard *Midway* alive.

The next morning, Blackburn shocked the crew when he climbed into the captain's chair on the bridge. His eyeballs were bright red from broken blood vessels and he had two world-class black eyes. No one dared asked the skipper how he felt. He was back on the bridge and that was that. Captain Blackburn lived life on the edge and loved it.

Fate soon tested that attitude. The day after *Midway* arrived in Pearl Harbor in 1958, mainland China launched a massive artillery attack on 100,000 nationalist troops on the Quemoy and Matsu islands. *Midway*'s stay in Hawaii was cut short when the Navy ordered it to head toward the Chinese conflict as soon as possible. Within a few weeks, the USS *Midway* again was patrolling between the two Chinas.

"Men, this is the captain," said Blackburn as *Midway* neared China. "In a few hours, we will be on station and within range of artillery on the mainland. Be ready, stay sharp, and know this: if we are fired upon it will be the start of World War III. I know *Midway* is ready. I know each of you is ready. Good luck. That is all."

The crew didn't know that Blackburn and his officers were preparing for a possible attack on China, including nuclear strikes on major cities. Millions of people could be killed. The Soviet Union likely would defend China if America attacked. Blackburn wasn't exaggerating about a possible World War III.

Captain Blackburn earned the respect of his sailors through his willingness to take risks and by making their welfare his top priority. *Midway*'s most popular captains generally were more accessible than most and were genuinely committed to crew morale.

Midway sailors called the Soviet spy ships that frequently followed the *Midway* battle group "tattletales." Ship trash was bagged in a special way to make sure it sank, so that the Soviet ships could not recover and search it.

One night, the order to attack nearly came. The pilots of the VAH-8 squadron reported to their ready room, where they were briefed on missions. VAH-8 pilots called themselves "The Fireballers" because they flew the aircraft that carried nuclear bombs. Commander Hal Woodson stood perfectly still as he scanned the faces of his pilots. The silence lengthened as they shifted in their seats. Woodson took a deep breath and told his men that orders to attack a Chinese airfield could come at any minute.

"Here's what I want you to do," he told them. "I want everyone to write his last letter home. Right now, before you leave this room. No excuses. Give me your letters. Those of you who come back will get their letters back. I'll mail the letters of those who don't return."

After each pilot finished his letter and handed it to Woodson, he headed to his bunk in search of sleep. He lay down fully dressed in his flight suit, a pistol at his side. If the call came at dawn, time could

Sometimes officers sent *Midway* pilots on extremely dangerous missions, knowing there was a very good likelihood that some would not return. Pilots occasionally were ordered to write letters to be delivered to their families only if they were killed in action.

not be wasted getting dressed. The call never came. The sun rose and routine air operations resumed. Perhaps someone in Washington had changed his mind about attacking China. After a sleepless night, the pilots of VAH-8 were never told why. They all got their letters back as *Midway* remained on station and routine patrols continued.

Meanwhile, President Eisenhower played a game of chicken with China's Chairman Mao. USS *Midway* aircraft patrolled along the coast while other Navy ships protected American supply ships bound for Quemoy and Matsu. Just over the horizon, Soviet warships cruised in wide circles. Finally, on October 6, 1958, China agreed to stop shelling the islands if the U.S. Navy stopped accompanying civilian supply ships.

As the crisis eased, the USS *Ranger* arrived to take over for the USS *Midway*. Before *Midway* left the area, a *Midway* helicopter pilot paid a visit to the *Ranger*, dropping a can of paint that splattered across the *Ranger*'s flight deck. An attached note said, "Our captain can beat up your captain." Its mission completed, the USS *Midway* left Chinese waters for the second time in four years.

Although Captain Blackburn's assignment as commanding officer of *Midway* soon ended, his reputation cast a long shadow over what became known as the "Disaster Cruise" commanded by his replacement, Capt. James Mini. He was the opposite of Blackburn. Some skippers commanded with a passion for accomplishing the mission; others commanded out of a fear of failure. Mini reflected the latter. Sailors winced at Mini's arrival on the bridge. They said his body odor filled the confined space.

By an odd quirk of assignments, Blackburn remained on board as chief of staff for the admiral on *Midway*. The USS *Midway* never sailed alone: it was surrounded by a group of ships that provided protection. The admiral and his staff on *Midway* were responsible for the entire battle group, while the captain was responsible for *Midway* and its crew. Some sailors called *Midway* "the mother ship" of the battle group.

Blackburn's popularity with the crew haunted Mini. One night, as an officers' party filled most of the hangar deck, two sailors headed for shore on liberty. As they tried to cut across the hangar deck, an ensign barked at them to take the long way around. Gene Coulter and Don Lockwood were more than a little irked. As they navigated the detour, one of them reached up and opened a valve that activated the overhead hangar-deck fire sprinklers. The officers' party came to a water-soaked halt as Mini sputtered in anger.

"That's my boys!" Blackburn laughed a few tables away.

The USS *Midway* never sailed alone. Accompanying ships defended the carrier. In addition, thousands of shore-based sailors who were specialists in maintenance, repairs, supply, personnel, training, safety, and mission planning supported every *Midway* deployment.

But Mini's greatest fear soon would become reality. He would confront one of the biggest crises ever faced by any *Midway* skipper.

Cotton-white clouds drifted across Subic Bay in the Philippines on November 9, 1959. *Midway* rested. Most of the crew was ashore on liberty, and only a faint hum vibrated through the ship. The exhaust fans' drone sounded as though *Midway* was breathing.

A frantic shout shattered the lazy morning. "Fire! Fire! In the after-heath pump room, fifth deck!" Men assigned to damage control rolled out of their bunks and broke through chow lines on their way to their emergency stations. Others, on duty in offices, repair shops, and engine rooms, barely listened, paused, and went back to work. Small fires were common aboard aircraft carriers.

Minutes passed.

"All hands. All hands. Abandon ship. Abandon ship. Report to the pier immediately."

Even on an all-steel aircraft carrier, fire was a primary concern. *Midway* carried millions of gallons of explosive fuel, hundreds of bombs and missiles, and dozens of nuclear weapons. Fire was the biggest threat to nearly all of them.

More than one thousand men flinched and then ran. They thundered down passageways, jumped through hatches, and scrambled up ladders. Above them, thin hints of smoke rose out of ventilation shafts near the island. Then it turned black and thick as it mixed with the outside tropical air.

Below, damage-control parties sprinted through the smoke, looking for the cause. Some had strapped on facemasks, while others ran through the poisonous, gray haze to join a fire-hose line. Sooty oil and sweat soon soaked sailors' faces, bare arms, and white T-shirts, turning them coalminer black. Suffocating heat watered men's eyes inside scratched facemasks as they walked into the smoke. They found the fire inside a compartment where equipment pumped jet fuel. Few locations on *Midway* were more inaccessible—few were more dangerous.

Not far away, Dick Singer gathered *Midway*'s secret codes, manuals, and messages. Singer had been a ham radio fan since junior high school. As soon as he graduated from high school, he and three buddies enlisted in the Navy so he could work in the communications department. *Midway*'s secret documents must be destroyed or taken with them if Singer and the rest of the crew abandoned ship.

"You think we're going to abandon ship?"

"Dunno."

"Maybe the tugs will pull us out of Subic."

"Focus, people. Pull your materials together and wait for orders."

Singer asked for permission to help the men who already were falling in the fight against the fire. Several had choked into unconsciousness. He ran down deserted passageways with a metal litter, looking for sailors who had collapsed from heat exhaustion. Singer's boots echoed through what had become a smoldering, smothering ghost ship.

Not far away, another closed world existed on *Midway*. More than two dozen men worked with its guided missiles. The GM Division was located directly above the fire. Captain Mini ordered damage-control parties to flood the missile compartment before it got so hot that the missiles began exploding. As this and several other ammunition compartments were flooded, the hours passed and the smoke continued to pour out of *Midway*. Men stood on the pier with axes in hand, ready to cut the ship loose in case it had to be towed out of the bay.

Admiral Blackburn and Captain Mini had to rely on thousands of *Midway* sailors to do their jobs in every emergency. In times of crisis, the aircraft carrier's most senior officers sometimes depended on some of the youngest crew.

Firefighters battled the fire for eight hours before they brought it under control. Decks cooled as night fell on the Philippines. Almost immediately, a damage-control crewman, Phillip Cunningham, was arrested. Cunningham had come under suspicion of setting several *Midway* fires because he frequently was the first on the scene once the fires were discovered.

Captain Mini was furious. The implications of arson on crew morale, his career, and the ship's safety were enormous. Mini ordered his legal officer, Barney Cochran, to sign the complaint as the accuser against Cunningham: justice would be swift. But as legal officer, Cochran was the ship's prosecutor in legal proceedings. He couldn't be the accuser, too. He tried to explain this to Mini but the captain wouldn't listen, even though it was a clear violation of the military's criminal-justice rules. Cochran, a law-school student when he had enlisted in the Navy, reluctantly signed the form. Several years after Cunningham had been sentenced to jail, he was freed "on a procedural technicality." The USS *Midway*'s most notorious firebug became a free man.

Cunningham had violated the trust that the crew had placed in him. Trust and teamwork are crucial aboard an operating aircraft carrier. If one man or department fails to complete an assignment, the lives of others are at risk. That is especially true on the flight deck. When any of *Midway*'s 200 pilots were on final approach to landing, they placed their lives in the hands of a single man: the landing signal officer (LSO).

"I just wanted to thank you. You saved my life last night." Many *Midway* pilots said this to the LSO at least once. The LSO stood on a platform at the back and to the side of the flight deck. Turning his back to the bow, he faced each incoming pilot as he approached *Midway* from behind. The LSO used his radio to coach every pilot to a safe landing at 150 miles an hour. Although *Midway*'s flight deck

A crash on the flight deck could be the result of mechanical failure, weather, poor communication, or crew error. Every time they landed, pilots trusted hundreds of men who otherwise were strangers on *Midway*. When accidents occurred, specialists had to repair the aircraft and sometimes manufacture parts at sea.

had grown to 1,001 feet long, the landing area where a pilot's tail hook must catch an arresting wire was the size of a tennis court.

"Okay, looking good," he would say. "Now a little power, you're low. Power, power! That's enough. Good. Mind your angle, nose up, tail down. Good, good."

The conversation was always one sided. A pilot never talked back to an LSO, other than to acknowledge he had the carrier in sight and to report his fuel status.

One night Vern Jumper, the son of a Los Angeles albacore fisherman, had LSO duty. Jumper was one of the best pilots in his squadron. He told engaging stories and had a face that quickly broke into a smile. On this night, an F-8 Crusader turned toward

Every pilot relied on "Paddles," the landing signal officer who stood next to the landing area and helped them land safely. Pilots landed at speeds of up to 150 miles per hour in a space the size of a tennis court.

the carrier in the dark and dropped too low early in his approach. The deck rolled back and forth in heavy seas, which made landing especially dangerous. Jumper told the pilot to give it power, but he stayed low for a full five seconds. Jumper told him to give it lots of power, forget the landing, go around, and try again. There was no answer. The pilot stayed low and kept coming. Then he drifted left, directly at Jumper. The LSO leaped into a safety net just as the pilot slammed into the back of the USS *Midway*. The fuselage sheared off equipment that Jumper had been using a few seconds before. The pilot died instantly. A feasible explanation of the crash eluded Jumper. That night stayed with him a long time.

Sometimes the LSO's judgment and the flight-deck crew's

The development of nuclear weapons and jets posed unique challenges. Nylon barricades first designed for propeller-driven planes sometimes failed to stop out-of-control jets. In this instance, the two men at the edge of the flight deck jumped out of the way before the pilot crashed into the parked aircraft and was killed.

teamwork weren't enough to avert disasters. One night, another Crusader pilot practiced landing on the angled deck while other pilots got ready to take off from the bow. The pilot hit the flight deck so hard that his plane broke apart. He ejected just as his wrecked aircraft slid over the side of the ship.

Vines Haughan was on duty as the officer of the deck up on the bridge. He watched the tragedy unfold. He noticed sparks erupting from a plane almost ready to take off, only seconds after the crashed Crusader had fallen into the ocean. The launch was canceled as rescue crews searched the waters for the pilot. He wasn't found.

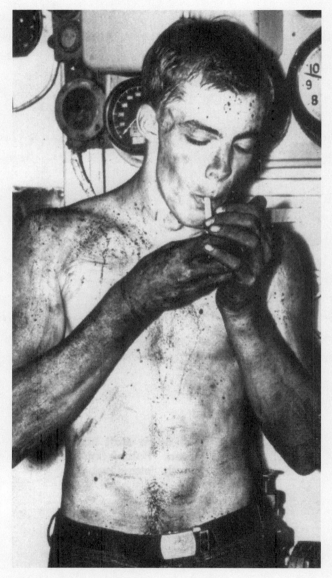

There was a time when some supervisors gave fifteen-minute breaks only to sailors who smoked. More than one sailor took up smoking in order to get those breaks, only to regret it later in life.

The next day, Haughan paid a visit to sick bay. He thought the pilot in the plane about to launch might have been injured when his plane erupted in sparks. Instead, the pilot who had crashed the Crusader looked up at Haughan. When the pilot ejected, his parachute had floated him over the flight deck and onto the aircraft ready for takeoff. He slammed into the plane, breaking bones. The jet engine's intake then sucked in the pilot's parachute, producing the sparks that Haughan had seen on the darkened flight deck. A chief petty officer had sprinted to the Crusader pilot's aid and cut the parachute's lines just before the jet engine would have swallowed the pilot. The Crusader pilot attributed his good luck to "the Almighty." Haughan agreed.

The USS *Midway* completed its last peacetime cruise in May 1964, when it tied up to a pier in Alameda, California. Nearly twenty years of endless drills and practices, more than fifty thousand landings, threats of war, and unpublicized skirmishes had come to an end.

Midway's next mission would become one of combat, dictated by battle plans against an unseen enemy. *Midway*'s crew prepared to sail into war for the first time.

Chapter 4

Combat Crusaders

The United States became deeply polarized in the 1960s. Opposition to America's involvement in Vietnam deepened and at times became violent. Thousands of young Americans were being drafted into military service with the likelihood of fighting in Vietnam. Some volunteered for the options that enlistment offered. Others fled to Canada to avoid military service of any sort. The civil-rights movement crystallized deepseated racial hatred as America struggled to reconcile a national vision of equality with the reality of inequality.

The USS Midway *was a microcosm of the United States. Its crew was a cross-section of America's ethnicity, political orientation, and values. As the United States struggled with its role in Vietnam, rampant drug abuse, and racial tensions, so, too, did* Midway*'s officers and young crew.*

Against this backdrop, Midway *sailed into combat for the first time after nineteen years of endless patrols under the threat of war.*

The sun beat down on the *Midway* attack jet's canopy as it thundered just above the North Vietnamese jungle treetops in 1965. Suddenly rifle fire erupted from a clearing. Bullets pounded the A-4 Skyhawk. It nosed over and corkscrewed toward the ground. Seconds later it exploded inside the Vietnamese jungle.

Ocean spray lifted up and over *Midway*'s bow before settling on M. D. McMican's World War II-era Skyraider. He and three crewmen sat

Midway pilots on bombing runs relied on sailors at radar stations back aboard the ship. Those sailors monitored the skies for enemy aircraft and directed rescue aircraft to remote spots in the jungle if a pilot was shot down.

poised on a catapult, ready to launch a rescue mission. The lives of the two USS *Midway* Skyhawk pilots who had crashed might hang in the balance. Maybe they had ejected before their jet exploded.

Soon the Skyraider circled over the crash site. A wispy column of ash-gray smoke drifted up out of the jungle. An invisible enemy took aim on McMican and his crew. Bright red tracers slammed into the Skyraider's fuselage. McMican struggled to control the aircraft as enemy fire found the plane a second time. He turned the crippled plane for the frantic race back toward *Midway.* Then the death spiral began. The jungle rushed up at the four young aviators inside. One managed to eject seconds before the Skyraider crashed and burned on the North Vietnam coast. He free-fell into the sea. His parachute never opened.

"Attention, this is the captain." Capt. James M. O'Brien had lost six young pilots in less than an hour.

Midway sailors on duty paused as they looked up at the nearest loudspeaker. Most knew nothing of what had happened seventy-five miles away. Captain O'Brien gave them the word. Some men gasped. Others sat down, their eyes suddenly watery. Many wiped a grimy sleeve across a forehead, sighed, and refocused on their jobs. Grief could not be allowed to interfere with *Midway*'s mission. Pilots got ready to fly the next combat mission of the day. Bakers, electricians, supply clerks, boiler tenders, and bomb-elevator operators went back to work. The routine of combat operations was relentless. *Midway*'s 4,300 sailors had to do their jobs so that the carrier's 200 pilots could fly their missions.

Pilot Dave "Tic Toc" Martin was one of them. The nickname came from the huge watch he wore as well as his passion for being on time. He had been a newspaper reporter before going to Navy flight school. He spoke in soft, measured tones and was immensely popular.

Martin learned to spot the clues to an especially dangerous mission during preflight briefings. Unusual emphasis was placed on "safe areas," rescue procedures, and the "120 rule": if you take fire and have to get out, put your plane on a 120-degree heading. Almost always, that will be your shortest route to the ocean. Water improved a pilot's slim chance of surviving a crash, which was far better than crashing in the enemy's jungle.

Midway pilots fought politics as much as the enemy.

"Hey, lookit down there! Those are MiGs on the ground. Let's go get 'em!"

"Are you nuts? No way! Rules of engagement say they have to attack us first."

"Yeah, but . . . "

"Button it."

Politically inspired "rules of engagement" required *Midway* fighter pilots to wait until they were fired on before they attacked the enemy. If the enemy approached Martin's jet, he had to make a visual identification, report it to *Midway* by radio, and then wait for permission to fire. By then the enemy might have established a superior firing position. *Midway* pilots complained they had to be

A pilot on *Midway* relied on hundreds of strangers every time he flew a mission: mechanics, aircraft-maintenance crews, weapons handlers, flight-deck personnel, and even the young men who attached rockets, missiles, and bombs to his plane.

lawyers to understand who or what threat could be attacked and under what circumstances. "It's like I'm fighting with one hand tied behind my back," one grumbled.

Midway pilots also rolled their eyes when they learned of bombing restrictions imposed by politicians who defended the war in the face of increasing public opposition. The politicians wanted only the most obvious and preferably isolated military targets attacked to minimize civilian deaths. Bridges were important targets, but nothing could be bombed within a mile of the Red Cross symbol. So the

Relentless combat missions exhausted both pilots and the ship's crew. Sailors cherished rare opportunities to take a break and perhaps sunbathe at the back end of the flight deck.

North Vietnamese painted red crosses on their bridges. The rules prohibited *Midway* pilots from attacking enemy missile sites under construction that would be firing at them in a few weeks. The sailors fumed that their pilots couldn't eliminate a potential threat before it turned deadly.

The best *Midway* officers were especially frustrated, including Bill Franke. He was an "old man," having become a pilot seventeen years earlier. On *Midway*, he planned missions and submitted them all the way up the chain of command to the Pentagon for approval. Many were denied for fear of civilian casualties. It was as if the enemy had immunity from *Midway* pilots.

On August 24, 1965, Franke flew high above a North Vietnamese bridge, watching for enemy aircraft, as the weather turned sour. Suddenly the enemy fired a telephone-pole-sized missile at his plane. It burrowed into the F-4 Phantom, exploding only a second after the crew ejected. Franke and his copilot, Robert Doremus, descended under parachutes into the jungle. Out in the Tonkin Gulf, air-traffic controllers on *Midway* knew that Franke's Phantom had gone down.

Deep inside the carrier, Ron McPhail and Oscar Granger sat in front of radar scopes. The clammy air stuck to their orange-tinted skin in a darkened room where red lights glowed. Both young men were radar operators. They tracked *Midway*'s aircraft to their targets and guided them back to the ship. McPhail was an Army brat who had enlisted in the Navy ten days after he had seen a Navy movie starring John Wayne. He was tall, thin, and wore his hat down low over his eyes. Granger stood just as tall, with a face that always held a hint of a smile. The country boy had fled South Dakota's cornfields when a Navy recruiter promised duty in San Diego.

McPhail and Granger were among the first to know when a *Midway* pilot had been lost. Sometimes their job became mechanical. First, they tracked the outbound planes on radar. After waiting from ninety minutes to four hours, they picked them back up on radar and monitored their return. They tallied the score of those who didn't return, focusing on numbers instead of men's lives. Emotion couldn't interfere with snap search-and-rescue decisions that might save a pilot's life or put rescuers' lives in danger. McPhail and Granger knew it didn't look good for Franke and his crew. Time for reflection would come later.

Within minutes of landing in a rice paddy, Franke and Doremus

In combat, radar operators had to develop a detached approach to their jobs. They were the first to know when a pilot had been shot down and crashed. But they couldn't let that bother them as they focused on the rest of their job.

were captured and taken to the North Vietnamese "Hanoi Hilton" prisoner-of-war camp. By 1965, it held hundreds of American prisoners. For most, days of pain ran together as the calendar blurred: pain at the hands of the enemy, pain of powerlessness, and the pain of imagining what wives, children, and parents must be enduring back home.

Perseverance and faith were as important to the *Midway* POWs as they were to the crew when they rolled out of bunks sticky with tropical sweat and mildew every morning. *Midway* combat deployments drained everyone. They typically lasted a month, followed by a one-week break in port for liberty and resupply. It was a gut-wrenching schedule of twelve-hour shifts. It was made even worse by the jobs some sailors performed.

Midway had two, seventy-five-yard-long, steam-powered catapults next to each other on the bow. Each contained a shuttle that connected to the front of the plane being launched. The shuttles accelerated massive aircraft from a standing start to 150 miles per hour in three seconds. Tremendous steam pressure drove each shuttle and the plane attached to it. It was as if *Midway* had a huge, double-barreled shotgun built into its flight deck.

Rick Janes, a skinny youngster from Minnesota, had to squeeze into the steam-catapult canals just below the flight deck. He had the bizarre job of cleaning the entire length of the catapult canals, which were barely large enough for a man to crawl through. In sweltering tropical humidity, Janes covered his body from head to toe with overalls, shirts, and gloves to keep all skin from touching blister-hot steel. Whenever he squeezed into a canal, a chief petty officer stood nearby and insisted that Janes keep talking as he worked. That way, the chief knew Janes had not passed out from the heat.

"Janes, you okay?"

"Yeah."

Deep inside the ship, young sailors were responsible for controlling the steam that drove *Midway*'s massive engines. The carrier's top speed was fast enough that a sailor could have water-skied behind the 70,000-ton ship.

"Janes! Are you all right? You still breathin' in there? Speak up, son!"

"Yes sir!"

Below deck, the heat sucked the energy out of a man as jets thundered overhead. For most sailors, the only relief from the brutal heat and humidity was talcum powder—pounds of it. Without it, itching became unbearable, and rashes spread like wildfire. The smell of sweat and talc drifted through the passageways.

Midway's awesome power was generated far below the flight

On occasion the smallest sailors in the Engineering Department were ordered to crawl inside pipes, vents, and catapults to make repairs. Sometimes they were ordered to keep talking while they worked, so their supervisors could be sure they hadn't passed out from the heat.

deck and even below the waterline. Twelve massive boilers fed four turbines that each loomed two stories high. The turbines drove the four, twenty-ton propellers. Pipes were barely recognizable under countless layers of insulation and dozens of coats of paint. The goal was to prevent any pinhole leak, as the high-pressure invisible steam would cut off a man's arm in a second.

The engine rooms deep inside *Midway* felt closer to hell than the wet air that swept across the flight deck. Heat hung in the air, drifting up through open metal grates that separated one level from the next. Thick paint on the walls became soft to the touch in the heat. Body odor blended with the smells of grease, steel, and rubber. Yet many compartments remained spotless. There were no oily footprints. Dozens of white-faced dials sparkled. The brass telephone handsets shined. Men cleaned equipment every day while wearing headsets that protected their hearing. The growling rumble of equipment echoed off whitewashed walls, entered a man's heels, and rolled up his legs. Raw, hot power humbled the young men responsible for its control.

Elsewhere, duty was just as tough. *Midway*'s galleys produced 13,500 meals a day to feed 4,500 men. More than five hundred fresh-baked pies were necessary for every sailor to be served one slice. It took more than four thousand pounds of beef for one serving each at a single meal. If mashed potatoes were on the menu, 2,000 pounds of potatoes had to be peeled. *Midway* sailors ate ten tons of food every day. Galley conditions were so hot and steamy that the cooks had trouble with mold and mildew—it grew in the hair on their arms because a shortage of fresh water limited showers.

Dominic Finazzo thought he knew something about heat. He was born in the North African desert and grew up in Brooklyn. When he was younger, Finazzo went to church every Sunday and sometimes swiped a candy bar along the way. When his Boy Scout troop visited an aircraft carrier, Finazzo knew right away he wanted to join the Navy. He never dreamed he would assemble bombs. A routine day for Finazzo consisted of using a hammer and chisel to loosen the frozen nuts on 250- and 500-pound bombs in humidity that made his hands and tools slick with sweat.

Midway sailors usually saw only about 20 percent of the ship during their entire time aboard. A sailor worked only a few yards from where he lived. Unless his job was on the flight deck, he might not see daylight for a week or more. The only way he could tell the time was when the ship's interior lights were turned red from 10:00 P.M. to 6:00 A.M. The dim lights did little to help him sleep, especially when he was new to the ship.

Sweat dripped off the faces of hundreds of men every day aboard the USS *Midway*. When air conditioning was added to the ship, it was for one reason: to cool the compartments that housed newly installed computers.

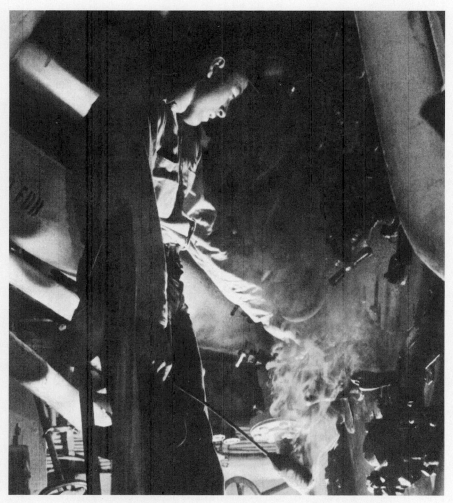

Sailors were not allowed to explore *Midway*. They were frequently told, "If you have no business there, you have no business being there." That included the flight deck, so many men went weeks without seeing the sun.

An aircraft carrier is noisy all the time. Solid steel carries clanks, clunks, and thuds throughout the ship. Sailors could feel the four ship turbines' vibrations in their feet. Sometimes they flinched when a 40,000-pound aircraft slammed down onto the flight deck. When mechanics fired up F-4 Phantom engines on the hangar deck or fantail to test them, a thunderous roar seemed to fill every compartment. Too, sailors were moving throughout the ship all night long. Like a hospital, *Midway* functioned twenty-four hours day.

Midway and its crew kept up the brutal schedule for months before it finally came time to return home. A blanket of fog brought tears to some men's eyes when the carrier again approached California's Golden Gate Bridge on November 23, 1965. They were home after having launched combat aircraft more than 11,500 times.

Once again, *Midway* needed a major overhaul to keep pace with advances in naval aviation. As preparations were made in late 1965 to put the carrier into dry dock for a four-year modernization, the skies over Vietnam quieted. The U.S. suspended bombing during the Christmas holiday season. The North Vietnamese took advantage of the lull. They rebuilt many bridges and facilities that *Midway* pilots had destroyed. Some were targets that *Midway* pilots had paid for with their lives.

Midway's reconstruction ultimately created a national controversy. Some Navy officials thought the original estimated cost of $88 million was excessive for a twenty-one-year-old ship that might last only another five years or so. But the Navy proceeded with the overhaul. Workers cut through steel every 4 or 5 feet all along *Midway*'s 1,000-foot hull. Electricians installed new electronics systems. Extensive work was completed in more than 1,300 compartments.

After three years of construction, *Midway*'s crew returned in late 1969. The following year, the carrier would be ready to go to sea. But in the meantime, *Midway* sailors faced open hostility when they

In the course of forty-seven years of service, *Midway* underwent several overhauls to accommodate new technology. When the carrier was built, computers had not yet been invented. Yet by the time it was retired, it relied on satellite communication.

left the Navy base to visit downtown San Francisco. Opposition to the Vietnam War was widespread and heartfelt. Many Americans took out their frustrations even on sailors who had been drafted into military service. Many sailors had decided to serve their country and risk death rather than flee to Canada to avoid being drafted. Some people even took shots at the entry-gate booth to Hunters Point, where *Midway* sailors were stationed. It became so dangerous that sailors were not allowed to leave the base on foot. Hunters Point was aptly named.

Midway sailors learned it wasn't wise to wear their uniforms on liberty in San Francisco. But since they weren't allowed to have civilian clothes on base, many of them rented lockers over a

Most sailors served about two years on *Midway*. The constant turnover required senior officers to train new arrivals in the intricacies of their jobs at sea.

downtown clothing store for quick changes. Some wanted to look like civilians so badly that they wore men's wigs to hide their short hair. The protests intensified. Four months after *Midway* returned to sea in 1970, members of the Ohio National Guard shot and killed four college-student antiwar demonstrators at Kent State.

The final price tag to complete *Midway*'s overhaul totaled $202 million. It was a huge price, considering that the aircraft carrier's complex power plant wasn't even touched. Supporters said that the Navy now had a nearly all new ship sitting on a relatively young twenty-five-year-old hull as young men prepared to take *Midway* back into combat and unimaginable danger. The families of those missing in action or presumed captured by the enemy five years earlier

Six years of significant modernization projects enabled *Midway* to serve for forty-seven years. The ship became part of the waterfront (top, right) near San Francisco during its most extensive overhaul (1966-70). Cost overruns and delays made the project nationally controversial but enabled *Midway* to serve an additional twenty-two years.

continued to pray, wonder, and weep. Soon, new families would have plenty to worry about.

October 24, 1972, had been another long day of flight operations off the coast of Vietnam. Every ninety minutes for twelve hours, aircraft had been launched and recovered. The flight-deck crew's arms hung heavy with fatigue. Sometimes the sailors stumbled in a cloud of exhaustion. Only one aircraft remained in the air, an A-6 Intruder. Tony Dennig watched the last landing of the night.

Dennig had enlisted in the Navy four years earlier. He had left Spring City, a small town in southeastern Pennsylvania. He had grown up in a river valley of rural communities, horse farms, rolling hills, and woodlands filled with deer.

Dennig watched the Intruder roar onto *Midway*'s flight deck. In a split second, the landing gear broke apart. It sent the Intruder into a sideways slide toward seventy-five men and thirty parked aircraft.

"It's coming! It's coming!" screamed Dennig as he pulled himself out from under a plane he was working on.

Flight-deck workers had no time to run across the four-acre deck to safety. The Intruder slid into another plane and broke in two. Flaming jet fuel spread across the flight deck and erupted in a red ball of flame. Small pieces of airplane tore into sailors' faces, chests, and arms. Dozens of corpsmen, the ship's doctors, and others raced to fallen sailors who were writhing on the deck. Only a few yards away, firemen stood at the edge of billowing red fire and shot fire-retardant foam at its base. Deeply personal emergencies littered *Midway*'s flight deck.

Four sailors died that night. More than two dozen fell seriously wounded. Jet fuel blinded one. Several required emergency surgery in *Midway*'s sick bay. A helicopter flew Tony Dennig ashore for an operation. He had been knocked more than thirty feet through the air from where he stood when the Intruder first hit the deck. When he woke up in the hospital in South Vietnam, he discovered he had suffered five broken ribs, two cracked vertebrae, temporary paralysis, a leg wound, and a punctured lung.

A day after his emergency surgery, a Navy notification team drove up the Dennig driveway in Spring City, Pennsylvania. They may have had news about a son who served in the Army, fighting in Vietnamese rice paddies. Or maybe they brought bad news about another Dennig son who flew helicopters in combat. Instead, they told the Dennig family that Tony had survived a horrible crash on *Midway*, he had been flown off the carrier with serious injuries, and they had no

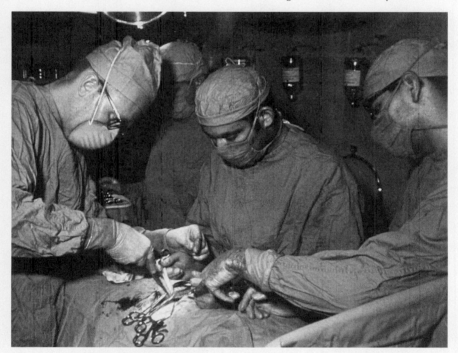

The hospital on *Midway*, called "sick bay," housed two operating rooms, an X-ray room, intensive-care unit, pharmacy, and eighteen hospital cots. Most sailors who were ill or suffered minor injuries were sent back to their bunks after treatment.

other immediate information. Like so many others, the Dennig family would have to wait and worry as *Midway*'s war continued half a world away.

Meanwhile, the aircraft carrier alternated between long combat assignments off the coast of Vietnam and short stays in California to replenish and train new sailors. In the spring of 1972, the decade-long war in Vietnam crumbled with a single invasion of South Vietnam by 120,000 North Vietnam soldiers. The communist army from the north stormed through villages on its way toward the South Vietnamese capital, Saigon. If they reached the city limits, the U.S.-supported South Vietnamese president might have to resign. Unification of South and North Vietnam under a communist government now appeared inevitable.

The USS *Midway* left its Alameda, California homeport on April 10 and sailed west toward Vietnam once again as fast as possible. The sailors faced more combat at a time when they struggled with simply being sailors. In the early 1970s, the United States ended the military draft. Public opposition to the war had grown so strong that few young men volunteered for service. As a result, the Navy loosened some of its strict regulations.

Veteran *Midway* sailors soon started complaining about the new recruits. Thefts aboard increased. Some new sailors had criminal records. Drugs use rose, just as it did in the U.S. In the early 1970s, the Navy discharged 5,000 sailors a year for drug use, compared with only 150 in 1966.

Midway's doctors grew overwhelmed by the personal issues of their sailors. The ship's Dr. Donald Vance asked that a psychiatrist be assigned to the aircraft carrier. (The request was denied.)

Dr. Vance had graduated from the University of Arkansas before joining the Navy. Tall and imposing, he had bright eyes that smiled. Vance expected various epidemics to sweep through the overcrowded ship. On one occasion, a sudden flu outbreak sent 800 sailors to sick bay. Outbreaks of sexually transmitted diseases, though, could be predicted almost to the day. After leaving some ports, the medical staff always expected a massive STD outbreak and made sure they had a large supply of antibiotics.

Monitoring the health of pilots posed different challenges. Even a

Privacy is a distant memory on an aircraft carrier. Sailors from across America had to learn how to work and live with all types of people. They had no choice of whom they worked with or who was assigned to their sleeping quarters.

cold potentially put a plane's crew in danger. A clear head was critical when flying a jet faster than the speed of sound. The same held true when aircraft were "shot" off *Midway*. Launching off the bow strained both plane and pilot. Pressure twice the weight of gravity pinned him against his ejection seat. His cheeks flattened and vision blurred. When he left the flight deck, he flew only fifty feet above the water. A pilot had only seconds to take control of his aircraft and lift the nose ten degrees. Then he brought the landing gear up, raised the flaps, and flew his mission.

A pilot must be in good health to withstand the tremendous physical strain. Pilots generally have large egos and are extremely competitive. Few admit to not feeling well. It was up to *Midway*'s medical staff to spot an ill aviator. One trick was to sit in the back of the ready room when a group of pilots was watching a movie. When a doctor heard a cough or sniffle, he asked the pilot to step out into the passageway for a private conversation. Few pilots argued with a doctor's judgment when he put him on the "down list" as unfit to fly. The stakes were too high, the margin of safety too narrow.

Each pilot—and sailor—made decisions every day about his work and how to conduct himself. Poor decisions sometimes killed. A single pilot relied on hundreds of mechanics, flight-deck personnel, catapult operators, and others. If one sailor failed to do his job, that pilot could die in a second. Sometimes the decisions made at sea by sailors on *Midway* haunted them for a lifetime.

Pilot Ray "Buzz" Donnelly had been a polite and stellar athlete at Villanova University. He once held an American swimming record. On occasion, he crouched under the wing of a plane to hand wrenches to a mechanic. He took time to explain his missions to aircraft electricians. He wanted everyone to know how they helped meet *Midway*'s mission.

One day, Donnelly and Mike McCormick flew a mission over

North Vietnam. As they prepared to attack their target, a handful of bullets ripped into their A-6 Intruder. Some of them found the cockpit. One pierced Donnelly's neck. McCormick was horrified. His plane's canopy was shattered, his cockpit covered with Donnelly's blood. McCormick flew back to *Midway* as fast as he could, screaming into his headset that Donnelly was badly hurt. He flew with one hand as he reached over with the other trying to keep the blood from flowing out of Donnelly's neck.

Dr. Vance got the word. In minutes, a plane would land with a critically injured pilot.

Ready rooms aboard *Midway* were private clubhouses for the pilots. Some pilots felt they were more important than the ship's crew, although the ship's commanding officers worked hard to develop a sense of unity and teamwork.

Sailors, especially the flight-deck crew, had to be extremely alert. While most landings were routine, mishaps tended to be sudden and unanticipated, such as a Sidewinder missile breaking free of a plane and skidding across the flight deck. Vigilance, despite exhaustion, was vital.

Sometimes it was sheer luck that a pilot survived a flight over enemy territory. He couldn't control whether enemy fire struck a vital part of his aircraft or passed harmlessly. Pilots sometimes were amazed at the damage suffered by their aircraft that continued to fly.

"Get me a forklift with a pallet on it!" he ordered a corpsman. "Now! You, get us up against that plane *before* he comes to a stop. You, get up here with me and hang on. No matter what you see inside the cockpit, I want you to secure the ejection seat when we get to the cockpit. Ignore what you see or smell. Secure the cockpit!"

McCormick somehow brought his plane aboard *Midway* in a haze of splattered blood. In seconds, Vance and his team were at Donnelly's side. It was too late. Too much blood had been lost. Donnelly slumped in his seat, dead from a few rifle bullets on their way up from the jungle toward the clouds.

On many occasions, *Midway* pilots were able to return to the carrier and land safely after being hit by enemy gunfire. Sometimes the damage was so large that a sailor could crawl through a hole in the wing or fuselage.

McCormick climbed out of the plane, white with shock. Then the nightmares began. He had seen enough and decided to tell the flight surgeon he was finished with flying. Maybe that would end the nightmares. Dr. Vance sat McCormick down for a long talk. They discussed life and death, perspective and purpose. In time, Mike McCormick decided to keep flying. He rejoined the endless cycles of launches and recoveries. He tempted fate by flying through enemy fire as peace talks dragged on between the U.S. and North Vietnam.

Six months later, another two-man Intruder crew headed toward a heavily forested North Vietnam valley dotted with surface-to-air missile sites. More than a dozen missiles rose to meet the American attackers. Undeterred, the bombers pounded the target, turned, and headed for *Midway* in the Tonkin Gulf. The Intruder never returned.

No one had seen it hit by enemy fire. Rescue crews retraced the route of attack and return. They searched hard for four days. They found nothing. The Intruder had disappeared without a trace, so the Navy listed the two-man crew as missing in action. One was Robert Alan Clark, a funny guy from Los Angeles. He had not yet met his son, who had been born after *Midway* had left California. The other pilot was Mike McCormick, the aviator who had decided to keep flying. He kept flying long after there was any hope that America could win the Vietnam War. He kept flying when pilots simply hoped to survive until the end of the war. He kept flying right up to the moment he was shot down—only seventeen days before the missile sites fell silent when peace was declared in Vietnam. Today, Dr. Donald Vance still thinks about Mike McCormick, devotion to duty, and honoring promises made.

The spring sun burned through the fog and warmed San Francisco Bay when *Midway* arrived in Alameda in 1973. Thousands welcomed the exhausted sailors. The war had ended. On *Midway*'s last combat deployment to Vietnam, two dozen shipmates did not come home. Many had been killed, some were missing, and others had been confirmed as prisoners of war. Another month passed before *Midway*'s ten POWs returned to the U.S. Some had been captured only a few months earlier. Pilot Jack Ensch spent a relatively short seven months as a prisoner of war before he was freed. Four others, though—Phillip Butler, Richard Brunhaver, Bill Franke, and Robert Doremus—somehow managed to survive at least seven years under filthy and near-starvation conditions before they were finally released so they could return to their families.

Every man on *Midway* had sacrificed in his own way, below deck, up "on the roof," in the sky, and even in a prison camp. With the war

Sacrifice came in many forms aboard the USS *Midway*. If a Skywarrior crashed into the sea, even alongside the carrier, it was nearly impossible for the crew to escape from the underwater fuselage before it sank to the bottom of the ocean.

over, each man and his family navigated a personal course out of harm's way toward home and inner peace. Some got there. Many faced nightmares for the rest of their lives.

Fresh young men replaced most of the veterans on *Midway* in the months following the Vietnam War. At the same time, international tension shifted away from Southeast Asia toward the Middle East. *Midway* would be assigned new missions. It would become the first Navy aircraft carrier homeported in a foreign country to be closer to world conflict and crisis. *Midway*'s sailors would chart a course through détente with the Soviet Union, the end of the Cold War, and the onset of terrorism. It began one night when thousands of frightened Vietnamese families stormed *Midway* in what became the Vietnam War's final chapter.

Chapter 5

Cold War Warriors

By 1975, the United States and the Soviet Union had waged an undeclared Cold War for nearly thirty years. The world had become a giant chessboard. They moved and counter-moved their forces, positioning their armies and navies (including the USS Midway) *to threaten attack or to block the enemy's advance. Conflicts escalated into crises in the Mediterranean, Korea, the China coast, Southeast Asia, and Cuba.*

The rise of terrorism and fervent nationalism in the Middle East in the 1970s created new players in world affairs. Egypt, Lebanon, Syria, Iraq, Iran, Afghanistan, and others became more militaristic. Long-simmering ethnic and religious hatred escalated into surprise attacks and regional wars between enemies that were small, sometimes invisible, and nimble.

Americans faced new and unexpected threats to world stability. The longstanding war of nerves between two superpowers was complicated by emerging threats elsewhere. A delicate, high-stakes game of brinksmanship with familiar and unknown enemies would define life at sea for the crew of Midway.

Vern Jumper gazed out toward the water from his post high in the island on the USS *Midway* on April 29, 1975. The carrier had been ordered back to Vietnam, two years after the last American soldiers had come home. The civil war had continued as North Vietnamese troops advanced toward and then reached the outskirts of the South

Vietnamese capital, Saigon. Now, the sea and sky both were blackish gray, merging at a horizon that smelled of defeat.

As air boss, Jumper practically lived in primary flight control, high in the island overlooking the flight deck. A small man with a head that looked too big for his slight build, Jumper often planted his hands on both hips while talking to several people at once. An FM radio headset that creased his crew cut enabled him to communicate with the men on the flight deck. He held a UHF radio to talk to pilots in the air. Within arm's length was a phone, which provided a direct line to the captain. Jumper's eyes constantly swept the fight deck from stern to bow and back again.

The air boss was responsible for everything that took place on the flight deck of the carrier. Fueling aircraft, positioning them for takeoff, and recovering them were all filled with danger. Safety was most important, followed by efficiency. Being air boss was one of the most demanding jobs in the Navy. Many sailors said the air boss also had the most unforgiving job on the ship.

Just before eleven o'clock that April morning, Armed Forces Radio played "I'm Dreaming of a White Christmas." That was the signal to start the final evacuation of American officials from South Vietnam. *Midway* helicopter pilots immediately rose off the deck and headed for Saigon.

Jumper thought about counting the black specks suspended just below the heavy cloud cover. It was impossible and didn't matter anyway.

Soon *Midway* would be surrounded by dozens of unauthorized helicopters. Their pilots intended to land either on the flight deck or in the sea next to the carrier. It would be up to *Midway*'s crew to rescue hundreds of refugees inside them before they drowned. The Vietnam War was over. All that mattered now was survival, either on a wet flight deck or in the Tonkin Gulf.

The air boss, responsible for all flight-deck operations, also had to know the status of emergencies below deck. Many men believe that the air boss has the most pressure-filled job on the ship.

Midway's flight-deck crew approached one helicopter designed to carry twelve Marines that had just landed. When they opened its side door, they pulled fifty small children out of it and onto their feet. Parents who stayed behind had stacked their children on top of each other like firewood for the sixty-minute flight to safety aboard *Midway*.

The refugee flood continued hour after hour. *Midway* sailors worked through the night to bring aboard 2,074 refugees in the first twenty-four hours. One out of ten needed immediate medical attention. Sailors gave up their bunks so fleeing brothers and sisters could stay together.

Midway sailors rescued more than three thousand refugees when South Vietnam was taken over by North Vietnam in 1975. Operation Frequent Wind was the largest helicopter evacuation in U.S. Navy history.

Midway's last mission in the waters off Vietnam, called Operation Frequent Wind, had been an act of the defeated. But it also rescued 3,073 refugees in nearly two days of continuous flight-deck operations. As sailors took the last refugee below, air boss Jumper began to relax. When he finally left primary flight control, he heard something he couldn't believe. This father of three young children listened to the sounds of infants aboard his warship.

Midway would embark on future humanitarian missions. They would offer welcome relief from a relentless war of nerves against the Soviet Union.

"The Soviets have lock-on!"

Midway's darkened combat-information center, where sailors scanned the ocean and sky with radar, came alive. The intermittent sound of a Soviet guided-missile cruiser's radar had turned constant. Were the Soviets about to attack from only 1,500 yards behind *Midway*?

For several days in August 1976, *Midway* and other Navy ships had sailed off the Korean coast, with Soviet Union and Chinese warships not far away. Tension had built up to a point where few men slept. Days earlier, two American soldiers cutting down a tree in the demilitarized zone between North and South Korea had been killed by North Koreans using axes and rifle butts. Called Operation Paul Bunyan, the U.S. Navy's increased offshore presence was a warning against further aggression by North Korea.

Radar operator Tom Utterback immediately reported the Soviets' lock-on signal to the captain. Capt. Larry Chambers didn't hesitate. He ordered two F-4 Phantom jets into the air immediately. He ordered a flashing-light message to the Soviet ship demanding it turn off its radar. Minutes passed as the Phantoms circled high overhead and waited for instructions to attack. Finally the radar squeal stopped and the Soviet cruiser drifted away from *Midway*'s course.

Courage and compassion are part of serving aboard an aircraft carrier. Most carriers complete humanitarian missions throughout their service life, where sailors and officers help people in need.

Sometimes Soviet bombers tested *Midway*'s capability of detecting their approach as well as its ability to launch aircraft in response. Here, a *Midway* pilot kept a close eye on a Soviet bomber as it flew almost directly over the carrier.

The carrier returned to its mission of sailing at the "tip of the sword." That had begun three years earlier, when the USS *Midway* became the first American aircraft carrier homeported in a foreign country.

Navy ships had been stopping briefly in Yokosuka, Japan, for more than twenty years. When the Vietnam War ended in the early 1970s, American military planners believed that rising Middle East tensions posed the next threat to world peace and stability. But the Indian Ocean lay on the opposite side of the Earth from Navy bases in the U.S. Steaming at a brisk twenty knots (twenty-three miles per hour), it took a carrier almost a month to travel from San Diego to the Persian Gulf. (In the early 1950s, when the Cold War centered on

Europe, *Midway* sailed from Norfolk, Virginia, to the Mediterranean in only ten days.) Creating a permanent homeport for *Midway* in Japan greatly improved Navy responsiveness in the face of a sudden Middle East crisis. Not everyone welcomed *Midway* to Yokosuka, though.

More than twenty thousand Japanese demonstrated against the ship when it arrived in October 1973. They claimed that a permanent U.S. Navy presence would lead to increased aircraft noise, unruly behavior in bars, and more serious crimes. Opponents also didn't want *Midway* carrying its nuclear weapons into port. (It had been only twenty-eight years since the U.S. had dropped nuclear bombs on Hiroshima and Nagasaki in World War II.)

Duty on *Midway* now meant living in a foreign country instead of returning to port in the United States. Sailors faced a new traffic system, suffocating road congestion, and a language barrier. Nearly three thousand *Midway* sailors were not married. When they returned to port in Yokosuka, there were no families or girlfriends waiting to greet them. Assignment on *Midway* now required extended separation from loved ones in the U.S.

Young sailors coped with the loneliness in different ways. At sea, privacy disappeared when a sailor slept in a compartment with hundreds of other men stacked in bunk beds. Letters and photos from home became precious. Sailors pasted them to the bottom of the bunk above them. They spent long off-duty hours staring up at photos of families, pets, girlfriends, cars, or maybe a favorite fishing trip with Dad. Family stories played out over weeks and months. It usually took at least ten days for a letter sent from the U.S. to reach *Midway* and a sailor's reply to reach home. If the first letter held bad news, *Midway* sailors frequently had to wait two weeks to find out whether the doctors decided to operate on Mom or whether she was still in the hospital.

It got worse once *Midway* transferred to Japan. It became known as the "USS *Neverdock*." In its first six years there, thirty-one deployments to sea were each separated by only about a month in port. As tensions increased between the U.S. and the Soviets in the late 1970s and early 1980s, American foreign policy dictated frequent and highly visible patrols by *Midway* throughout the Western Pacific and Indian Ocean.

"You see this? Helo's off course. Where's he going?"

"Don't know!"

Midway's helicopter pilot had received orders to change both his course and radio frequency. The orders came from a voice with a Texas twang. It was an easy voice to listen to—down home and genuine. *Midway*'s crew jammed their helicopter's alternate frequencies until the pilot finally returned to the designated *Midway* frequency. That's when he learned he had been following flight instructions from a Soviet who spoke English with a Texas accent!

Sometimes *Midway*'s contact with the Soviets took place at the edge of space. *Midway* officers knew that low-orbit Soviet satellites

Confrontations between *Midway* pilots and Soviet aircraft during the Cold War were almost never publicized. Reporters were not embedded on *Midway,* as they often are on ships and with ground troops today.

tracked every *Midway* movement. One of *Midway*'s classified experiments captured the signals sent by the Soviet satellites and returned fake signals with misinformation about *Midway*'s location and direction.

Electronic war games with the Soviets exhausted *Midway*'s combat information center crew. Sailors sometimes sat at their radar scopes for twenty hours at a stretch, tracking as many as twenty Soviet ships. With only eight hours between shifts, a radar operator could spend an hour and a half waiting in the chow line to eat or instead get as much sleep as possible. Most preferred the extra sleep and tried to get by on a Snickers bar and cup of coffee when the Soviets were nearby.

They knew that most exercises against Soviets tested who could spot the other first. In the nuclear era, the first punch in a war of missiles at sea probably would be a knockout. Radar enabled *Midway*

During extended combat and shipboard crises, *Midway* sailors were allowed to take brief naps wherever they could. The ability to get to sleep quickly and not be bothered by an extremely loud environment was an asset aboard an aircraft carrier at sea.

to locate other ships and aircraft in the area, but it also enabled other ships to locate *Midway*. To keep the Soviet Union from tracking *Midway*, sometimes the carrier ran EMCON: sailing without sending radar signals to search the sea and sky. But without radar, *Midway* steamed blind.

Midway was a giant black hole moving through the Strait of Malacca between Sumatra and the Malay Peninsula the night of July 29, 1980. Its radar operated at the minimum setting. The escorting destroyers used "deception lighting" to create a nonmilitary ship profile. On its way into the Indian Ocean, *Midway*'s battle group tried to elude the ever-present Soviet ships that were following the armada.

Some sailors became more religious and sought counsel from the ship's chaplain in times of great stress. Danger, uncertainty, marathon deployments, and months away from family took a toll on officers and sailors.

Duty on the flight deck could be brutal. Sailors worked eight hours or longer. Some were loaded down with aircraft chains on a deck that rolled in the waves and in a wind of close to thirty miles per hour if flight operations were under way.

Not far away, a Panamanian freighter called the *Cactus* that was filled with telephone poles sailed on a parallel course. At about eight o'clock, *Midway*'s collision alarm suddenly sounded. Men jumped at the noise. As the alarm blared, *Midway* lifted out of the water and listed hard to starboard. Sailors' eyes widened in horror as a deep, grinding growl rolled through the ship. Terror spread on *Midway* as the carrier settled back into the water.

"Battle stations! Battle stations! Man your battle stations—set condition Zebra!"

The freighter had changed its course and rammed *Midway*. It tore three ten-foot holes in the side of the ship. It ripped apart planes at the edge of the flight deck and destroyed an oxygen-making plant just below. Within seconds, jet fuel flowed from the broken planes onto the flight deck and down into the plant, which was also leaking liquid oxygen. The mixture seeped down into lower compartments that contained guided missiles. If it caught fire, *Midway* could blow up.

Midway sailors focused on their emergency duties. Usually when an emergency was declared, each sailor ran to his emergency duty station and then stood around until the training drill or minor emergency such as a trashcan fire was resolved by others. Sailors trained for emergencies almost every day. They had to memorize their destination and responsibility if "General Quarters" sounded, as well as different responsibilities for other emergencies such as collisions or abandon-ship orders.

Randy Kittilson ran to the combat information center and heard "secure to abandon ship." He started throwing reams of top-secret codes, manuals, and other documents into a safe that would sink to the bottom of the sea. Brian Pellar had dropped out of a Los Angeles high school before joining the Navy. Assigned to nuclear weapons, he had taken extension courses on *Midway* and earned his high-school degree. On this night, he sprinted through abandoned passageways deep in *Midway* to make sure the sea wasn't pouring into the compartments that contained the nuclear bombs.

One of the most important groups in a crisis was the communications personnel. With sailors spread out through 2,000 compartments, communication was vital in order for everyone to receive orders and work together.

Up on the flight deck, the chaotic scene shocked a sailor who maintained weapons on the aircraft. John Morris had been struggling in the Navy. He was having a tough time dealing with *Midway*'s officers, who went by the book and didn't hesitate to punish a sailor if he stepped out of line.

Spilled jet fuel was spreading across the flight deck. Missiles attached to the wings of damaged aircraft now were lying on the deck in pools of extremely flammable jet fuel. Morris and others ran toward the soaked missiles and threw themselves onto the deck. Lying on their backs in caustic jet fuel, they held their breaths as they

With jet fuel leaking near missiles on the flight deck on July 29, 1980, *Midway* was in danger of a catastrophic explosion. Some sailors dismantled 500-pound bombs and pulled them away from the spill.

dismantled 500-pound bombs and missiles and pulled them away from the fuel. The biggest threat to *Midway*, missiles and bombs exploding in jet fuel, had been eliminated.

Nearly five hours after the collision, safety and order had been restored aboard *Midway*. Sailors staggered to their bunks, utterly exhausted. Most didn't know that Daniel Macey and Christian Belgum had been killed where they stood, working in the oxygen-making compartment.

July 29 had become a night of fear, loss, and heroism. Danger always loomed on *Midway*'s horizon, as the Cold War with the Soviet Union continued into its fifth decade. As new threats emerged in different parts of the world, *Midway*'s officers confronted both new and familiar enemies. Sometimes they were baffled when old foes ignored *Midway*.

Grigori, a Soviet fisherman, walked out onto his fishing pier along the Soviet Union's east coast one morning. He instinctively ducked as roaring jet aircraft from the USS *Midway* and USS *Enterprise* dove out of broken clouds toward the pier. They were part of three American carrier groups totaling forty warships that had assembled near Grigori's fishing grounds off the Kamchatka Peninsula. It was the largest collection of American warships since World War II. They had planned a naval exercise that they hoped would prompt the Soviets to send their newest bombers out to observe. The U.S. Navy wanted to get a look at the new Soviet Backfire bomber.

The Soviets, though, ignored the Americans. Two years later, the Navy discovered why. For more than fifteen years, John Walker, a Navy communications specialist, had been selling Navy codes to the Soviets. They had been reading *Midway*'s electronic mail.

Spies always worried the Navy. Since *Midway* was homeported in a foreign country, the Naval Intelligence Service agents kept a close eye on *Midway* sailors. Agent Ken Lord sailed with *Midway*. He spoke with a sharp, purpose-filled voice. He solved crimes and watched for possible spying activities. Ultimately, two *Midway* sailors were caught as Soviet spies. Food-service worker James Wilmoth convinced Russell Paul Brown to collect secret documents that usually were burned. Wilmoth planned to sell them to the Soviets, but both were caught. Wilmoth was court-martialed and sentenced to thirty-five years at hard labor (later reduced to fifteen years). Brown fared little better. His sentence was ten years in prison. The U.S. Navy dishonorably discharged both.

Although a KGB agent had recruited Wilmoth when he had been off duty, some men on *Midway* barely knew what off duty was. That included the captain of *Midway*. The leader of thousands of men in a floating city never rested. Some captains retreated under the pressure, while others thrived. The reputation of a few reached near-legend proportions, even with sailors who rarely saw their skipper. Two of those captains were aboard in the 1980s. Chuck McGrail was a large horse of a man who had been a good Catholic boy while growing up in Chicago. Sensitive about a receding hairline, he lifted weights with other sailors in the ship's gym. Another favorite was Riley Mixson, a thick-lidded Georgia native of average height with a soft Southern accent.

They were two different skippers who shared certain leadership skills that inspired young men from across the country. One trait was being available to the crew. McGrail was famous for inviting off-duty sailors up to the flight deck when a "green flash" might occur. (Under certain weather conditions, the sun setting on the ocean produces a flash of light that's emerald green.) Mixson took a different approach. He was well known for wandering the *Midway* at one o'clock in the morning, talking with butchers, bakers, and boiler tenders who worked the night shift on a ship that never stopped operating.

Commanding officers aboard the USS *Midway* lived under immense pressure. They had missions to complete, sailors to train and motivate, and the ship's safety to maintain and remained vigilant for possible spies and other security threats.

Toughness also was the hallmark of *Midway*'s most admired captains. One day, *Midway* turned into the wind to begin flight operations. A Soviet destroyer that had been tagging along suddenly changed course to force *Midway* away from the prevailing wind. An irritated McGrail decided to use a little backyard basketball strategy with his 70,000-ton warship. He ordered full speed and opened up a ten-mile lead on the Soviet destroyer. Then a Navy frigate slipped between the two as a "pick" to keep the Soviet ship away from *Midway*. Now free to launch aircraft, McGrail sent two F-4 Phantoms high over the Soviet destroyer. Then a *Midway* helicopter flew right up to the Soviet ship's bridge and hovered as a decoy. McGrail's "players" now were in place.

After a few minutes, the helicopter banked hard and departed just as the two Phantoms completed their dive at the Soviet destroyer

Even in a career of more than thirty years, most captains of the USS *Midway* said their eighteen-month command of the carrier was the unrivaled highlight. Every one of them marveled at the capability of the young sailors, most of them away from home for the first time.

from 20,000 feet. The sonic booms that exploded directly over the Soviets startled the Americans, who were ten miles away. For the rest of the day, *Midway* conducted air operations without interference.

Mixson, who had flown more than 250 combat missions in Vietnam, could be just as tough. His cramped at-sea cabin was only six feet wide and ten feet long. It served as bedroom and work station. A telephone sat between his thirty-inch-by-thirty-inch shower and toilet. It was cramped, Spartan, and functional. Three hours of uninterrupted sleep were a blessing in Mixson's world.

McGrail's and Mixson's natural camaraderie with their crew set them apart from other *Midway* captains. Their constant interaction with sailors formed the foundation of trust. *Midway* sailors believed that their skippers had the crew's welfare at heart. With trust came teamwork, efficiency, and a track record of accomplishment that became known as "*Midway* Magic." That standard of operation became critical in the face of unseen threats as *Midway* patrolled 100 million square miles of ocean.

By 1986, *Midway* was forty-one years old. Major improvements were needed for a third time, as aviation technology advanced at lightning speed. One issue was *Midway*'s famous tendency to roll hard from one side to the other, even in moderately high seas. The "USS *Rock & Roll*" required stabilization. Naval architects decided to lighten *Midway* and add hollow-steel compartments—called blisters—to the sides of the hull to make the ship more stable. Japanese shipyard workers went right to work on making the blisters. In addition, they removed 48 tons of weight by pulling fifty-six miles of unused cable from *Midway*'s overhead spaces. They eliminated another 300 tons by reducing the armor plating that protected the steering mechanisms at the back of the ship.

But only days before *Midway*'s anticipated return to sea, the carrier's officers received bad news. The ninety-two blisters had been rushed through testing. They reduced the ship's tendency to roll, but they also made the ship "snap back" to level too fast. That was very dangerous if air operations were under way. *Midway* remained one of the most difficult carriers in the fleet to land on. Some aviators were qualified to land on every carrier except *Midway*. In the meantime, even the new stabilizing blisters couldn't protect *Midway* from the typhoon of 1989.

The carrier steamed off the coast of Luzon as the typhoon approached. For more than twenty-four hours, *Midway* rode out the storm as waves pounded the hull and gale winds screamed across the empty flight deck. The crew leaned into each roll, first one side, then the other, for hours. Clammy faces whitened with fear. Relentless waves ripped off the antennas along the flight deck. Seawater rushed into the hangar bays before receding. As the carrier pressed ahead, word spread through the ship: *Midway* had survived a twenty-four-degree roll, eclipsing the legendary rolls of past deployments.

The crew joked that the next time *Midway* put in to port, a periscope would be installed on the bottom of the hull. That way, when the carrier finally rolled over and "turned turtle," the crew could find its way home. The leadership of *Midway*'s officers and the training of its crew had enabled *Midway* to survive the typhoon's horrors. That same training also enabled young men from Sacramento, Tulsa, and Raleigh to race into danger and risk their lives if it meant saving the USS *Midway*.

Jets thundered onto *Midway*'s flight deck in the Northern Pacific, 125 miles northeast of Tokyo, on the morning of June 20, 1990. At first, no one noticed that a storeroom full of pipes located three decks below a flight elevator was filling with smoke. As it grew thicker, *Midway*'s Flying Squad—a handpicked team of thirty men—was summoned. The Flying Squad was *Midway*'s first responder to almost every potential emergency. As often as 150 times a year, the Flying Squad handled poisonous fumes, toxic-substance spills, small fires, and false alarms. The Flying Squad represented the first-responding fire department of *Midway*. If they deemed a situation serious enough, the Rescue and Assistance (R&A) Team arrived as reinforcement.

After each flight, pilots reported all problems with their aircraft, so that repairs could be made before the next flight. During combat, each aircraft often was flown by several pilots on different missions in the course of a single day.

Jeffrey Vierra was a member of the Flying Squad. An office clerk in the repair division, he had volunteered for the extra assignment. His buddy, Joe Stalaboin, was part of the R&A Team. Stalaboin hardly noticed the alarm that had sent Vierra running. Then Stalaboin's R&A team was summoned.

"Maybe this is serious," thought Stalaboin.

When Vierra's Flying Squad reached the smoldering storeroom and opened the hatch, an explosion ripped through the men. It slammed them against each other and into steel bulkheads in the cramped passageway. The blast was so powerful that it blew a steel door off its hinges on the far side of a nearby galley. As the smoke thinned, blackened sailors writhed on the deck.

Stalaboin stopped to help an injured shipmate. He half-carried him to the main galley, where corpsmen had set up emergency treatment stations. Stalaboin choked at the scene. Human forms that barely resembled men lay on the steel deck. They were men who had shared his berthing compartment, eaten meals with him, and worked alongside him. Men were so badly burned that he recognized some only by the shape of their torsos. Their bodies quivered with pain. The smells of burned flesh, melted hair, asphalt, oil, smoke, and scalded steel all mixed together.

Almost an hour later, fire crews had regrouped and were attacking the fire when a second explosion roared through *Midway*. More injuries resulted. At that point, the firefighters retreated and grew cautious. Their mandate was always "don't let the cancer spread." Their job now was to keep the fire from intensifying. Meanwhile, men carried critically burned sailors up to the flight deck, where helicopters evacuated them to hospitals in Yokosuka, Japan.

Below deck, other young men kept fighting the fire. They used the ship's ventilation system to flood surrounding compartments with foam. They battled almost until midnight as the firefight turned into

Practice drills were a way of life on an aircraft carrier. Men trained endlessly for a variety of possible crises, in addition to performing their normal jobs. In case of a fire, every sailor could become a badly needed firefighter.

a marathon. Volunteers replaced exhausted firefighters. Some were so thoroughly spent that Marines carried them to a remote galley, where they peeled off smoldering clothes and breathed clean air.

Finally, in the early hours of June 21, *Midway* beat the fire. When firefighters entered the compartment where the first blast had occurred, they found the bodies of Jeffrey Vierra and Ulric Johnson. Nine others, seriously burned, had been flown off *Midway* for emergency care. One of them did not survive his wounds. The

Midway sailors had lost their lives because a corroded valve had failed in a relatively inaccessible part of the ship.

In an instant on *Midway,* routine, risk, and danger had become one. As the tide of détente rose toward the end of the Cold War, *Midway*'s life drew to a close. Four months before the fire, the Navy had announced that the forty-five-year-old *Midway* would be retired permanently the following year. Despite that decision, flight operations continued, men trained, and sailors responded when alarms sounded. Soon *Midway* would be handed two final missions. One would be to lead America into battle, and the other would be to rescue Americans thousands of miles from home.

Chapter 6

Seasoned Sailors

For nearly two generations, the United States had endured a Cold War with the Soviet Union. Massive buildups of nuclear weapons on both sides and the development of extensive and sophisticated espionage had produced a stalemate between the two superpowers. Outright war had somehow been averted.

Then the Soviet Union imploded. By 1990, its economy had collapsed under the weight of massive military budgets and a disastrous military intervention in Afghanistan. A groundswell of democracy swept reformists into power. The Soviet Union disintegrated as Russian republics gained independence. Communist dictatorships in Eastern Europe crumbled. West Germany and East Germany were reunified. The Cold War ended without the glory of victory. It simply died of exhaustion.

Meanwhile, tension and warfare intensified in the Middle East. Iran and Iraq fought for eight years. When Iraq's Saddam Hussein invaded oil-rich Kuwait, the United States mobilized against a new enemy.

Once again, young Americans aboard the USS Midway *and thousands of other sailors, soldiers, Marines, and Air Force personnel were called on to project American purpose and protect American interests.*

Terry Pudas felt he could reach up and touch the stars that blanketed the night sky late on January 16, 1991. The air boss stood in primary flight control high in the island as *Midway* plowed through the Persian Gulf. *Midway*'s always-present hum settled in his feet as Pudas looked down through the hazy red glow that covered the flight deck.

Knots of helmeted men seemed alien in the light. Reflective tape on their jerseys and muted flashlights gave them the appearance of leisurely fireflies in the night. Pudas was responsible for all the men on the flight deck. Just five months earlier, Saddam Hussein's Iraqi troops had invaded and occupied Kuwait. *Midway*'s flight-deck crew was poised to launch the first strike of Operation Desert Storm to liberate Kuwait.

Not far away on the bridge, Art Cebrowski sat in his elevated, blue captain's chair overlooking the flight deck. Many thought that Captain Cebrowski was among the brightest officers in the Navy. He had turned down more prestigious assignments for the opportunity to command *Midway* because of its past accomplishments. He promised his superiors that when Desert Storm started, *Midway*'s pilots would launch twice as many aircraft as the other larger, newer, and more powerful carriers. Cebrowski knew that *Midway* had set similar records in the Vietnam War. He believed that *Midway* sailors and pilots would do it again.

Mike Shutt sat in his F-18 Hornet, waiting for the order to launch at dawn. At 1:00 A.M. on January 17, 1991, Adm. Dan March on *Midway* received the message that began Operation Desert Storm: *launch the jets*. Shutt's jet canopy shuddered as one *Midway* night-attack jet after another thundered off the bow. Soon the departing jets' lights mixed with the stars, and a tense quiet returned to the flight deck. Operation Desert Storm had begun with *Midway* pilots leading the way toward two targets: an airfield near Basra in Iraq and a bunker in Kuwait suspected to contain chemical weapons.

At dawn, it was Mike Shutt's turn to face the enemy for the first time in his life. As his flight of attack jets reached the shore at the

Thousands of hours of training were put to the test every time the "shooter" touched his knee to the deck and pointed to the bow. Less than three seconds later, a 40,000-pound aircraft reached a flying speed of about 150 miles an hour.

speed of sound, an accompanying flight of Marine jets was supposed to fire a defensive rocket at enemy missile sites once every minute to protect *Midway*'s pilots. Missile contrails suddenly filled the sky. "My God," Shutt thought, "this is going to be a long war if those are all enemy missiles." They weren't. The Marines had spooked, firing all their rockets at once. *Midway* pilots pressed ahead, attacked their targets, and returned safely to *Midway*.

By the fourth day, jets from several American battle groups had destroyed nearly all of Iraq's surface-to-air missile sites. *Midway* pilots owned the air as they obliterated Hussein's communications equipment and then attacked troop emplacements in advance of the American assault on the ground. Around-the-clock flight operations drained sailors and pilots.

The pilot of an antisubmarine-warfare jet tried to land on *Midway* even though he was assigned to another carrier nearby. "Wave off! Wave off!" screamed the radio operator at the last second. The pilot had become so exhausted that he failed to notice that *Midway* had a different smokestack and smaller flight deck than his carrier.

Air boss Pudas wasn't surprised. He rarely slept more than fifteen minutes at a time in the early weeks of Operation Desert Storm. He napped on a cot built into the primary flight control ceiling. Shane Dulansky, a plane electrician working down on the flight deck, was equally exhausted. Only eighteen years old, he had wanted to join the Navy—just like his grandfather and uncle—since he was a little boy.

Often Dulansky found himself on the flight deck, his head inside a plane, frantically repairing a bad electrical circuit while his pilot

Tagging once was a Navy tradition. If a pilot landed on the wrong aircraft carrier, the flight-deck crew "decorated" his aircraft. When he finally returned to his carrier, it was his responsibility to clean off his plane.

During Operation Desert Storm, flight operations were so intense that the flight deck's asphalt covering was worn down to bare steel. *Midway* became the first carrier in the Navy to reapply the asphalt topcoat at sea and return to battle in a matter of days.

stood nearby, anxious to launch. After he turned the plane over to the pilot, JP-5 jet-fuel fumes would burn Dulansky's eyes. Walking behind a jet's roaring engine, he would drop his head so that grit from the flight-deck surface wouldn't dig into his face and eyes. The thrust of some *Midway* jets at full throttle while still on the flight deck was twice that of the strongest tornado ever recorded.

After six weeks of endless flight operations, mind-numbing exhaustion had become the Desert Storm enemy that threatened American lives at sea and in the air. More than 1,700 enemy tanks, 1,000 personnel carriers, and almost 1,500 artillery pieces had been destroyed when the American ground assault began. That offensive included a fake amphibious landing. *Midway* participated in the deception, navigating through 1,000 enemy mines in the Persian

Gulf near southeastern Iraq. *Midway* pilots bombed the coast as if Marines were about to come ashore. The ruse worked so well that nearly 80,000 Iraqi troops dug in to repel landings that never took place.

At 4:30 A.M. on February 27, sweat and body odor filled BK #10, one of the pilots' overcrowded bunkrooms. It had threadbare carpeting that smelled of mold. Cables, wires, and pipes covered the ceiling. It looked more like the inside of a boiler. The junior officers took a short walk from BK #10 to their ready room, where they would be briefed on their next mission. Their eyes widened and then locked onto the ready room's closed-circuit television's frozen picture. "Rejoice, We Are Victorious."

Desert Storm had ended. Peace had closed *Midway*'s final combat chapter. The aircraft carrier had set another naval aviation standard. *Midway* had flown more missions per aircraft per day than any other carrier. *Midway* made good on Captain Cebrowski's promise that the oldest and smallest carrier in the fleet would outperform all others.

A few months later, a spring sun warmed Philippine jungles and America's Clark Air Base. Only eight miles away, Mt. Pinatubo awakened from more than six hundred years' sleep. Steam billowed from the volcano's vents. On June 9, a column of ash shot into the air. The next morning, 16,000 Americans were told to abandon the air base and head for a nearby Navy base. *Hurry. Take no more than one suitcase. Leave your pets behind. The volcano might explode any minute.*

Maybe in a few days they could return. That faint hope disappeared only three days later, when the twentieth century's largest volcanic eruption took place. More than 1,000 feet of the 5,725-foot volcano vanished, leaving a crater a half-mile wide. As lava and ash rose twenty-two miles into the sky, a typhoon arrived. The tropical moisture mixed with the airborne volcanic ash. Thickened rain became wet cement that crushed everything it touched.

On what became known as "Black Saturday," sixty buildings collapsed. A gray, ashy snowfall deepened to a foot on airplanes. Electrical lines snapped under the weight of ash. A spooky, dusky light enveloped the frightened refugees as they hoped for evacuation. Meanwhile, USS *Midway* officers met in Yokosuka, Japan, to decide how they would rescue the homeless Americans on one last humanitarian mission.

Larry Ernst had taken over *Midway* only three days earlier in Japan as the ship's fortieth and last captain. He had penetrating blue eyes, a solid jaw, and a high-ridged nose. He was long, lean, and demanding. He had trained as a fighter pilot and looked like one. Ernst had joined the Navy after growing up in West Virginia's coal-mining country. He had decided there was more to life than going to work in a West Virginia coal mine or a steel plant in Ohio. By the time he became a commanding officer, he believed that "you get what you inspect, not what you expect."

Shortly after taking command, Ernst assembled his department heads to talk about the possibility of a rescue mission. Their response shocked him. His officers didn't wait for orders;, they immediately started planning the mission. Where would the evacuees sleep? How much food would they need? What about emergency medical care? Can we find diapers and pet food? A few days later, *Midway* steamed for the Philippines. The crew had amassed enough emergency supplies to last for up to two weeks for 5,000 refugees.

The Navy's relief force of twenty-two ships arrived on June 21, 1991. More than two hundred thousand people had been evacuated from their homes near the volcano. Thousands had fled to the Subic Bay Naval Base, where it had become nearly silent outside. The birds had disappeared. Every few minutes a "*c-r-a-a-a-c-k*" was heard as another palm tree collapsed under the weight of raining ash.

Thousands of frightened people stood on the pier at Subic where

Midway tied up. The heat was suffocating, and floating ash caught in the back of their throats. Most wore a T-shirt, shorts, and sandals and carried one suitcase. Slowly the line crawled into *Midway*'s massive hangar deck. They were amazed at what awaited them.

A *Midway* sailor greeted each refugee and escorted him or her to anything they needed. One end of the hangar deck had been converted into "Ernst's Eatery," where cooks served steak dinners. Others were taken straight to sick bay to see corpsmen and doctors. That night, more than 1,820 evacuees slept on *Midway*. Although they

After nearly five decades of service, *Midway*'s final mission was humanitarian. Sailors manned their emergency stations and prepared to rescue Americans fleeing the eruption of Mt. Pinatubo as it destroyed Clark Air Base in the Philippines.

had been told not to bring their pets, *Midway* welcomed twenty-three cats, sixty-eight dogs, and one lizard. For the only time in forty-six years, yaps, yelps, and meows could be heard aboard the USS *Midway*.

A few months later, Captain Ernst received a letter from a man living in Universal City, Texas. He had been rescued by *Midway* but had not met the captain. Part of the letter said, "What I witnessed [aboard *Midway*,] in my humble opinion, was above the extraordinary. . . . Let [your sailors] know that because of their example, if I ever encounter a U.S. sailor in need of any sort of assistance, no matter how inconvenient it might be, I will gladly render assistance and without hesitation. God bless and Godspeed USS *Midway*." It was written by an Air Force sergeant.

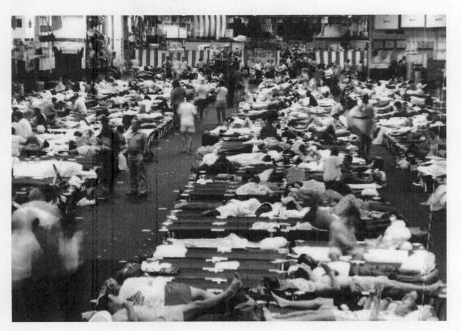

Midway's hangar deck was converted into emergency sleeping quarters for nearly two thousand evacuees following the twentieth century's largest volcanic eruption.

Near the end of *Midway*'s service life, its flight-deck personnel were responsible for making sure badly outdated equipment remained functional and safe. Flight-deck operations continued almost up to the day *Midway* was permanently retired.

Midway both saved and changed lives. Much of that had taken place while it was stationed in Yokosuka, Japan. After eighteen years of being based in a foreign country thousands of miles from the United States, it was time for *Midway* to come home.

Midway had become an institution in the Japanese culture. Thousands of Japanese shipyard workers had spent their entire careers maintaining and repairing the ship. Many rightfully felt that *Midway*'s accomplishments were partly due to their craftsmanship. Japanese fathers had taught their sons how to repair the increasingly complex machinery.

As helicopters followed *Midway* out of Yokosuka into Tokyo Bay one last time on August 10, 1991, the ship sprang a surprise on its adopted home. Nearly four hundred *Midway* sailors in dress-white uniforms assembled on the flight deck. Like a college marching

Diplomatic relations is one of many roles played by aircraft carriers and their crew. The USS *Midway*'s sailors forged a close relationship with the people of Japan when the ship became the first American carrier based in a foreign country. Some sailors' wives moved to Japan to be closer to husbands who served on *Midway*.

band, they stood shoulder to shoulder to spell "SAYONARA" for the news crews in the helicopters. The final USS *Midway* image on Japanese television showed its young men paying their respects to a country that some of their fathers had fought against in World War II almost fifty years earlier.

Midway's time had passed. Federal budget cuts required the Navy to reduce its aircraft-carrier force from twelve to ten. *Midway* had become too old to repair anymore. Newer, nuclear-powered carriers operated more efficiently. *Midway* had become too small and inadequate to handle massive new Navy jets. It was time to return home and step aside.

The old man shuffled toward two *Midway* sailors. He barely had the strength to walk up the ramp from the pier onto the ship after it arrived in Seattle. The sailors at the top of the ramp stepped forward and each took an elbow to help him aboard. A stained and ragged 1955 *Midway* cruise book was clamped under his arm. He was visiting his old ship for the first time in thirty-six years. He was crying.

The USS *Midway* had arrived in Seattle a few days earlier when a flawless sunrise greeted the sailors, making the snow atop Mt. Rainier sparkle. But the ship was destined for a dirty, industrial Seattle waterfront district for a three-day open house. *Midway* officers wondered who cared enough to go out of their way to see an old aircraft carrier. More than fifty thousand Seattle residents went out of their way. Several stopped the first *Midway* sailor they saw and simply said, "Thank you." Others came aboard one last time, years after they had served on the ship. Many told friends and family that "this is where I learned how to be a man."

Then it was time to leave for the city where *Midway* would be retired. On September 14, 1991, the ship turned into San Diego Bay. Off to the left were ominous black nuclear submarines floating in their pens. On the right side of the bay sat a Navy base on North

Island, where jets took off over the Pacific Ocean within sight of Mexico. The USS *Midway* would be decommissioned in a city fiercely proud of its Navy heritage. The first Navy pilots had learned to fly in San Diego Bay nearly one hundred years earlier.

Exactly forty-six years and four days from the moment *Midway* had

Midway was still a formidable fighting machine as it approached Pearl Harbor in 1991, where its aircraft would be transferred to the USS *Independence*. Less than a year later, *Midway* was decommissioned in San Diego.

joined the Navy fleet, it completed its last mission. As it settled alongside a NAS North Island pier, the time neared for the final departure of men, supplies, and equipment. Captain Ernst and his executive officer, John Schork, had six months to get *Midway* ready for permanent retirement. But first *Midway* had to go to sea for one last inspection.

The tests were brutal. Inspectors ordered full speed ahead and then emergency stop. Every piston, circuit, and pump on board measured up to the inspectors' demands. By day's end, *Midway*'s performance had shocked the inspection team. They found the ship still capable of service. On the bridge, an inspection admiral turned to Ernst and said, "We have two-year-old nuclear carriers that can't do all that *Midway* did today. Be proud."

"Does that complete the inspection, sir?" asked Ernst. It did.

The sun had set behind *Midway*, leaving a muted pink across the western horizon as the carrier headed back into San Diego Bay for the last time. The deepening, near-violet marine haze dimmed the city skyline dead ahead. An Indian-summer wind that swept *Midway*'s deck softened as the carrier approached the pier. *Midway* turned silent when the last sailor went ashore, proud of what his carrier had accomplished that day.

Ernst and Schork went to work, supervising crews that stripped *Midway*'s 2,000 rooms bare. Galleys that once prepared ten tons of food a day sounded hollow as countless pieces of cooking equipment were hauled away. Paper and ink were carried out of the ship's printing office, but the presses were left behind. They were too large to fit through the door. Medicines, patient charts, and X-ray films were hauled out of sick bay, while the X-ray machines and operating tables remained. Sometimes letters to sons and photos of wives were discovered in the corners of abandoned bunks:

As *Midway* was prepared for retirement, letters were found in the crew sleeping quarters. They reflected pride, a sense of duty, intense loneliness, newfound appreciation for the life back home, and uncertainty about what the future might hold.

Hi Son,

We love you and miss you a lot. It was sure nice talking to you. It was sure hot here today. It was real hot here yesterday. It has cooled down quite a bit since a couple of days ago. It won't be long before school starts. Dad goes on nights starting Monday, Aug. 31.

How come you will be out at sea only a few weeks? That seems like a short time. You sure are seeing the world. We got your letter and postcard today. It sure is pretty. How far are you from Tokyo? Have you ever rode the bullet train? Bet it would be fun to ride.

Our garden is just about all gone now. A few tomatoes left, but not many. Well, I will close for now and write when you have some time. We love and miss you a lot. Thank you for all the postcards. It is sure nice that you can send some home to let us see what it is like over there. Bye for now.

Love you very much and miss you,
Dad and Mom

As one compartment after another was cleaned out, the large hangar deck just below the flight deck merited special attention. That was where people entered the ship and the planes were maintained. Executive Officer Schork ordered sailors to polish every brass fitting and give everything a new coat of paint—make it sparkle for years to come. "Who knows?" thought *Midway*'s officers. "Maybe *Midway* would become a museum someday and be opened to the public."

December 24, 1991, was a silent night aboard *Midway*. Only a year earlier it had led the U.S. Navy in liberating Kuwait in Operation Desert Storm. Then it raced to the Philippines to rescue Americans from Mt. Pinatubo. Now *Midway* sat silent. A final goodbye loomed.

A puffy gray San Diego sky hung over *Midway* on April 11, 1992. As the morning sky lightened, three *Midway* pilots got dressed to say goodbye. Riley Mixson, the boy from Georgia who had grown up to become a captain of *Midway,* nervously paced back and forth. Mugs McKeown had become a famous *Midway* fighter pilot in Vietnam. His daughter answered the phone by saying, "McKeowns, home of the greatest fighter pilot in the world . . . who's calling?" The third was Dick Parker, who lived less than a mile from where *Midway* rested. He had flown aboard the ship on Halloween Day 1945. He was one of the first pilots assigned to *Midway*. The three aviators would join more than five thousand others for the ceremony to decommission the USS *Midway*.

Captain Ernst took a deep breath to calm the butterflies in his stomach as he stepped up to the microphone to begin the proceedings. He introduced the featured speaker, Adm. Robert Kelly, who was in charge of the Navy's Pacific Fleet.

"Born in war, she is retiring in peace," said Kelly. "That is an enviable accomplishment for any warship. While peace is closer than ever in our lifetime, the battle is not won." He was referring to the rise of terrorism in the late 1980s and early 1990s.

Captain Ernst shared a Mt. Pinatubo memory with the crowd. "When the refugees walked on board and into the bright lights of *Midway,* they were treated to a steak dinner and a cheery smile from *Midway* sailors. I've never been prouder of men under my command. I learned *Midway* Magic is not an empty catchphrase. *Midway* Magic is an amazing ability to excel . . . no matter what the odds."

As Captain Ernst stepped away from the podium to mark the ceremony's conclusion, thunder rolled out of the east. It developed into a powerful roar as four *Midway* F/A-18 Hornets passed only a few hundred feet overhead. They flew straight down the aircraft carrier's deserted flight deck and out over the Pacific. Precisely at noon on April 11, 1992, *Midway* Magic rested for the last time.

Several weeks passed before a seagoing tug secured a line to *Midway* to tow it up to the Navy's collection of retired ships in Bremerton, Washington. As the tug slowly pulled the carrier north along the Southern California coast, *Midway* reawakened. Even though its rudders were locked in place, *Midway* drifted to the west. That should have been impossible for a ship with no power or steering. It appeared to be drifting into the prevailing current, toward deeper water and, ultimately, Japan.

The crew on the seagoing tug was at a loss to explain it. Alarmed, they slowed and then resumed power. They watched carefully. After several minutes, *Midway* settled back in behind the tug, yielding to destiny.

The forty-seven-year odyssey had come to an end. In its wake, the world had forever changed. A Cold War had erupted, persisted for decades, and then died. Then followed the Korean War, showdowns with China, the Vietnam War, rescue missions, the jet age, the space age, the invasion of Kuwait, and terrorism. After more than seventeen thousand "Plan of the Day" editions, *Midway*'s final edition reflected an unmatched record of service to country by 200,000 young men:

After *Midway* (center) was retired, it was towed to Bremerton, Washington, where the Navy stores hundreds of ships of all types, either for possible reactivation or, more likely, permanent disposal.

Today we say goodbye to a proud warrior. As we leave, each of us will take our memories of Midway with us. I will remember the "Magic." For years I had heard of it, but never really understood. Having been on other carriers whose attitude was "We can't do that," when I got to Midway in January 1991 the real spirit of Midway hit me: "What can we do to make it work?" It was pervasive—everyone's attitude was—work together and we can do anything. In the last 16 months we fought a war, conducted a major evacuation, changed homeports, "aced" a final inspection, and smoothly decommissioned the ship. We did it safely and professionally. Yes, I will remember the "Magic"—you guys were the "Magic." It was a privilege to sail with you, best of luck in the future.

John Schork
Executive Officer
USS Midway

Twelve years after retirement, the USS *Midway* was relocated to Navy Pier in San Diego, where it opened as the USS Midway Museum in 2004. Thousands of *Midway* sailors have traveled from across the country to visit their former home one last time.

Conclusion

The latter half of the twentieth century perhaps was as fluid as any era in documented history. In a relatively short thirty years, world crises and conflicts shifted from Europe and the Western Pacific in the 1940s to Southeast Asia in the 1960s and then the Middle East in the 1970s.

In that time, the United States ordered millions of young Americans into uniform to defend their country. By the 1970s, America had come to rely on an all-volunteer military of high-school graduates, dropouts, and those intent on making the military their career. Today, the United States military competes with the private sector for young Americans, offering unparalleled education and career-advancement incentives. In World War II, young Americans were expected to fight and die for their country because it simply was their responsibility to do so. Today, young men and women serve after far more sophisticated training and with expectations of greater initiative and critical thinking.

Technology revolutionized service to America as well. In World War II, a young sailor was grateful for a letter from home every two weeks. Today, soldiers and sailors have e-mail accounts, post videos on the Internet, and watch family gatherings in real time. In the same seventy years, killing technology has evolved from World War II's M16 rifle to today's enemy tanks armed with satellite dishes and crews that can see and attack in the dark.

Yet as the mantle of military service has passed from one generation to the next, commonalities bind the young sailors, soldiers, and Marines of the 1940s with the young men and women in uniform today.

Teenagers, only a year or so past high school, remain capable of handling enormous responsibility. With the proper training and fortified by purpose and motivation, they complete assignments their parents would think impossible.

Too, they learn to embrace trust and teamwork and eschew individual glory. The aircraft-carrier pilot learns to trust strangers to maintain his plane properly and to correctly operate the steam-driven catapult when he launches on a mission. The sailor deep inside a ship learns to trust that boiler repairs were made correctly by an electrician before he ignites the boiler. The crew learns to trust the butchers, who ensure that tonight's beef on the menu isn't contaminated.

The odyssey of the USS *Midway* and the 200,000 young men who served aboard reflects the true capability of each generation as it takes its place in American society. *Midway*'s legacy also reflects the country's passage through the latter half of the twentieth century. As international and domestic priorities changed from the 1940s to the 1990s, so too did the expectations of young Americans aboard *Midway*. For example, the ship spent less than 10 percent of its service in open combat (Vietnam and Desert Storm). It spent more than forty years patrolling, protecting, and preserving in all kinds of conditions. At one point, it set a record of 327 consecutive days at sea. It achieved greater fame for its humanitarian missions than for its combat deployments.

Over forty-seven years, 213 young Americans made the ultimate sacrifice aboard the USS *Midway*. Some were buried at sea and others were brought home to their families. A few were never found before they sank to the bottom of the ocean or disappeared in a jungle. That, too, is part of the *Midway* legacy.

In the end, the USS *Midway* became a mosaic comprised of young Americans serving their country, usually asking for little in return when they came home. Today, many of them are plumbers, programmers, teachers, and even nuclear-power-plant operators. They silently served and sacrificed with courage and compassion. That, too, is the legacy of young Americans at sea.

Appendix

USS *Midway* Memorial List*
(Crewmembers lost during forty-seven years' service)

Name	Date	Notes
1940s		
William Anton Conrad, Jr.	1940s	
Philip Schubert Hofmann	1940s	
Harry Andrew March, Jr.	1940s	
AMMH2C James Story	1940s	
Harold Oakley Williams	1940s	
Frank McGuigan	Feb. 18, 1946	Drowned
ENS James R. Williams	May 15, 1946	Plane crash on deck after wave-off
AMM1 Hugh E. Williams, Jr.	Aug. 20, 1947	
James W. Lamm	Dec. 29, 1947	Helicopter pilot crashed in Naples, Italy
AMM2 Glenn P. Butler	Dec. 29, 1947	Helicopter crash in Naples, Italy
PFC Laird B. Darling	1947-48 cruise	Killed in a prop strike
Hershel Harold Donahue	1947-48 cruise	
William Louis DuCros	1947-48 cruise	
Jack Jeter	1947-48 cruise	
Chester Victor Truchel	1947-48 cruise	
James Russell Williams	1947-48 cruise	
Harry Duane Campbell	Feb. 11, 1948	Boatload of sailors and marines capsized
S1QM Albert Daniel Fisher	Feb. 16, 1948	Motor launch capsize in Gulf d'Hyeres, France
GM2 Vincent Geza Nemeth	Feb. 16, 1948	Motor launch capsize in Gulf d'Hyeres, France
MM2 Raymond Julius Poncel	Feb. 16, 1948	Motor launch capsize in Gulf d'Hyeres, France
MM3 Harold Williams	Feb. 16, 1948	Motor launch capsize in Gulf d'Hyeres, France

FA Lester B. Bohning	Jan. 8, 1949	Auto accident
AA George C. Heitman	Jan. 10, 1949	Accident
FN Wilford B. Murphy	Feb. 24, 1949	Accident

1950s

LT John J. Hale	1950s	
G. L. Leland	1950s	
J. J. Mazy	1950s	
G. H. Pearce	1950s	
ENS William R. Dinsmore	1950	Plane crash
AT3 Wyman I. Goodenough	Sept. 18, 1950	Plane crash
Charles Roger Babcock	1952	
Karl George Wenzel	1952	
LT James W. Ferguson	1953	
LTJG Hugh C. Hayworth	1953	
LTJG William J. Leonard	1953	
LTJG Guy T. Thrower	1953	
LTJG A.D. Foster	Jan. 10, 1954	
LTJG George Gleason	Mar. 31, 1954	
LT William Henry Paulsen	Mar. 31, 1954	
AN John Arthur Humphreys	Mar. 31, 1954	
LT William D. Henry II	May 16, 1954	
AT3 Charles George Schifflin	May 27, 1954	Aircraft landing accident
LTJG John Trumbull Lee, Jr.	May 27, 1954	
AE2 Arnold Julius Witzke	May 27, 1954	
AA John A. Brown	1955	
ADAN Bradford R. Darling	1955	
LTJG George M. Sostarich	1955	
LTJG A. J. Delano, Jr.	Sept. 7, 1958	Crash near Formosa
LTJG A. G. Bergevin	1959	
LTJG J. Brender	1959	
RM1 G. L. Harding	1959	
CDR W. H. Heider, Jr.	1959	
LTJG R. T. Johnston	1959	
LTJG J. D. Rivers	1959	
LTJG T. L. Williams	1959	
ADAN Joe H. Ingram	1959	

1960s

Maurice Eugene Hanson	1960s	
CDR George Veling	1960s	
Norman C. Fox	1960	
LT John J. Hale	1960	
LTJG Doulas A. Blank	1960	

LTJG Noel J. Stace	1960	
Frank J. Vallone	1960	
LTJG James R. Ward	1960	
AN John R. Brown	1961	
LTJG Robert J. Hendershott	1961	
1stLT Joseph S. Andre	May 3, 1961	Crashed on takeoff
CDR Charles Edward Guthrie	Dec. 12, 1963	
PT1 Joseph Edward Armstrong	1964	
ENS Joe Eddie Crosswhite, Jr.	1964	
ADJ3 Clyde Eugene Davis, Jr.	1964	
LTJG Ray Gordon English	1964	
LTJG Richard Lee Karns	1964	
LT Charles R. Mandly	1964	
ATCS Russell Marshall, Jr.	1964	
LT Ronald Samuel Sterret	1964	
CDR Richard McKenzie Tucker	1964	
LT Paul Michael Grafton	Oct. 17, 1964	
CDR James La Haye	May 8, 1965	Killed in action
CDR Doyle W. Lynn	May 27, 1965	Killed in action
LT John McKamey	Jun. 2, 1965	Killed in action
ATR3 William Harry Amspacher	Jun. 2, 1965	Killed in action
LTJG David Marion Christian	Jun. 2, 1965	Killed in action
ATR3 Thomas Lee Plants	Jun. 2, 1965	Killed in action
LTJG Gerald Michael Romano	Jun. 2, 1965	Killed in action
LTJG M.D. McMican	Jun. 2, 1965	Killed in action
LTJG Carl Louis Doughtie	Jun. 10, 1965	Killed in action
LCDR Harold Gray, Jr.	Aug. 7, 1965	Killed in action
LTJG Donald Hubert Brown, Jr.	Aug. 12, 1965	Killed in action
LCDR Francis Rogere	Aug. 12, 1965	Killed in action
LT Gene Gollahon	Aug. 13, 1965	Killed in action
LTJG Thomas Edgar Murray	Oct. 28, 1965	Killed in aircraft accident
AN Eddie Billups, Jr.	Nov. 3, 1965	Fell overboard, drowned
LCDR Arthur K. Tyszkiewicz	Vietnam War	

1970s

T. Bleuins	1970s
Bruce Flanary	1970s
LCDR Henry Benjamin Meyers, Jr.	1970s
Lannie Moss	1970s
ABH2 Charlie Curry	Feb. 2, 1971
LT Ellery B. Pearlman	Oct. 19, 1971
AT2 Roger E. Poe	Oct. 19, 1971
LCDR Keith L. Rasmussen	Oct. 19, 1971
LT Ned J. Tucker	Oct. 19, 1971

LT D. H. Vonpritchyns	Oct. 19, 1971	
CDR Charles E. Barnett	May 23, 1972	Missing in action
LT Raymond P. Donnelly	Jul. 19, 1972	
LTJG Gary L. Shank	Jul. 23, 1972	Missing in action
LCDR James L. Anderson	Aug. 8, 1972	Lost at sea
AZ1 Bobby Don Cobb	Aug. 8, 1972	
LCDR Michael W. Doyle	Aug. 25, 1972	Missing in action
LCDR Donald A. Gerstel	Sept. 8, 1972	Missing in action
AMH1 Edward P. McDonald	Sept. 13, 1972	
AN Robert W. Haakenson, Jr.	Oct. 24, 1972	
LTJG Michael S. Bixel	Oct. 24, 1972	Lost at sea
AO2 Clayton M. Blankenship	Oct. 24, 1972	
AMSAN Daniel P. Cherry	Oct. 24, 1972	
AA Robert A. Yankoski	Oct. 24, 1972	
LCDR Clarence O. Tolbert	Nov. 6, 1972	Missing in action
LT John C. Lindahl	Jan. 6, 1973	Lost at sea
LTJG Robert A. Clark	Jan. 10, 1973	Missing in action
LT Michael T. McCormick	Jan. 10, 1973	Missing in action
ADR3 William S. Stringham	Feb. 3, 1973	Lost at sea
1st LT USMC Jot Eve	Oct. 22, 1973	Plane crash
LTJG Everett E. Goodrow, Jr.	Oct. 22, 1973	
ADJ1 Richard H. Hall	Oct. 22, 1973	Plane crash
1st LT USMC David L. Moody	Oct. 22, 1973	Plane crash
LTJG William J. Bates	Oct. 22, 1973	
LTJG George A. Wildridge	Oct. 22, 1973	
LT Richard L. Pierson	Nov. 12, 1973	Plane crash
SD3 Feliciano C. Reyes	Dec. 31, 1973	
LCDR George P. Kroyer	Apr. 19, 1974	
William T. McIntosh	May 8, 1974	
Andrew A. Hill, Jr.	May 19, 1974	
LT James L. Feeney	Jul. 11, 1974	Plane crash
SA Daniel J. Lefevre	Sept. 13, 1974	
1st LT USMC Paul V. Duncan	Nov. 3, 1974	Plane crash
CDR Dennis C. Weeks	Aug. 20, 1975	Crash on takeoff
AA Pedro L. Morales	Dec. 24, 1975	
SA Ronald R. Cawein	May 18, 1976	
AM3 Stephen A. Felix	May 18, 1976	
AN Johnny A. Stefano	May 18, 1976	
GMSN Richard J. Zerbe	Jun. 5, 1976	
AG3 Jeffrey L. Hawley	Jul. 16, 1976	
AMH2 Bruce E. Flanary	Nov. 2, 1976	Plane crash
AME1 John S. Bates	Nov. 2, 1976	Plane crash
ADJ1 Roger W. Cook	Nov. 2, 1976	Plane crash
AOAN R. C. Knox	Dec. 1, 1976	Missing at sea

AMSAA Edgar Seth Moore, Jr.	Jan. 13, 1977	Lost at sea
LCDR William A. Counts	Mar. 30, 1977	Plane crash
ABF3 Lannie W. Ross	Jul. 16, 1977	Yokosuka Naval Hospital, Japan
ADR3 Andrew K. Ball	Aug. 25, 1977	Plane crash
LT Julian L. Moon III	Aug. 25, 1977	Plane crash
LT Charles R. Rhodes	Aug. 25, 1977	Plane crash
AZ2 Gary Lynn Morgan	Sept. 6, 1977	Yokosuka, Japan
ADR3 Randy Allen Blake	Sept. 16, 1977	Yokosuka, Japan
RM3 Thomas A. Cipriani	Feb. 26, 1978	Yokosuka, Japan
RMSN Mark H. Maciecki	Feb. 26, 1978	Yokosuka, Japan
AOC Jimmy Lee Davis	Aug. 16, 1978	Manila, Philippines
AT3 David James Zuidema	Aug. 25, 1978	Lost at sea
HTFN John Albert Cournoyer	Dec. 5, 1978	Pattaya, Thailand
ABF1 Leslie Cardell Taylor	Dec. 5, 1978	Pattaya, Thailand
AQCS Plummer Lee Rhodes	1979	
AA Lee Hampton Moore, Jr.	May 22, 1979	Yokosuka, Japan
AMEAN Joe Stanley Jones	Jun. 13, 1979	Olongapo City, Philippines
ABFAN Lawrence Morris	Sept. 7, 1979	Olongapo City, Philippines
SGT Roy Frank Kinzalow	Dec. 17, 1979	Lost at sea

1980s

ABE3 John Abboud Faries	Jun. 28, 1980	Yokosuka, Japan
MM3 Christian John Belgum	Jul. 29, 1980	Collision at sea
MM2 Daniel Francis Macey	Jul. 29, 1980	Collision at sea
LCDR Henry Meyers, Jr.	Nov. 4, 1980	Plane crash
Joseph Alexander McGibbon, Jr.	Mar. 25, 1981	Lost at sea
MRFA James Arthur Watts	May 5, 1981	Lost at sea
AK3 Enrique Talavera Lazarie	May 29, 1981	Auto accident
EM3 T. Blevins	Aug. 4, 1981	
LTJG John Muirhead	Aug. 29, 1981	
LTJG Stephen Mark Martone	Jun. 4, 1983	Lost at sea
Candelario Fuentes, Jr.	Nov. 30, 1983	Lost at sea
LCDR Timothy K. Murphy	Apr. 2, 1984	Plane crash
FN John Becerra	Jun. 16, 1984	Boat accident
AO3 Johnny L. Steel	Jun. 18, 1984	Yokosuka, Japan
LT R.J. MacFarlane, Jr.	Jul. 16, 1984	Plane crash
LTJG David M. Sperling	Jul. 16, 1984	Plane crash
AO2 Mark E. Todd	Jul. 22, 1984	Auto accident
LT Thomas R. Doyle	Aug. 21, 1984	Plane crash
AD1 Leo D. Ortiz	Nov. 18, 1984	Lost at sea
MMC Romeo Frias Cabrera	Apr. 2, 1985	Heart attack
LT Kevin R. Kuhnigk	Aug. 18, 1985	Plane crash at sea
ENS Christopher Mims	Aug. 18, 1985	Plane crash at sea
AN Robert S. Shaffer	Sept. 9, 1985	

AMSAN Steven E. Seitz	Oct. 20, 1985	
AN John Andrew Aguirre	Nov. 20, 1985	Lost at sea
EM2 Christopher Hayes	Jan. 5, 1986	Motorcycle accident
AA John M. Peyton	Jun. 8, 1986	Motorcycle accident
BTFN Curtis Jones	Aug. 16, 1987	Drowning accident
AW2 Joseph S. Pfleghaar	Nov. 9, 1987	Lost at sea
LT John Hatcher Carter	Nov. 19, 1987	Lost at sea
LT David A. Gibson	Nov. 19, 1987	Lost at sea
CDR Justin Noel D. Greene	Nov. 19, 1987	Lost at sea
LT Douglas A. Hora	Nov. 19, 1987	Lost at sea
HT3 Michael D. Knaus	Feb. 24, 1988	
AR Leslie W. Glenn	Apr. 13, 1988	
SH3 Enrique A. Escasa	Jun. 1, 1988	
LTJG Jay Kendall Cook	Jan. 28, 1989	
AT1 William A. Phillips, Jr.	May 30, 1989	Motorcycle accident

1990s

Leo D. Ortiz	1990s	
AFCN Madison Lavern Smith	Jan. 27, 1990	Respiratory failure
Joseph H. Courtney	May 11, 1990	Heart attack
MSSN Ulrich P. Johnson	Jun. 20, 1990	Flying Squad fire
DC3 Robert S. Kilgore	Jun. 20, 1990	Flying Squad fire
FN Jeffery A. Vierra	Jun. 29, 1990	Flying Squad fire
AKAN Anthony Terry	Jul. 30, 1990	
AMEAA Kevin J. Hills	Dec. 23, 1990	
AE2 Brian P. Weaver	Dec. 23, 1990	

USS *Midway* Aviators Who Became Prisoners of War**
(All returned home in 1973)

LT Phillip Butler	Apr. 20, 1965
LCDR Robert B. Doremus	Aug. 24, 1965
CDR F.A. Franke, Jr.	Aug. 24, 1965
LTJG Richard Brunhaver	Aug. 24, 1965
LT Aubrey A. Nichols	May 19, 1972
LCDR Gordon C. Paige	Jul. 22, 1972
LTJG Michael G. Penn	Aug. 6, 1972
LT John C. Ensch	Aug. 25, 1972
LTJG David A. Everett	Aug. 27, 1972
LCDR Theodore W. Triebel	Aug. 27, 1972

*Courtesy of ongoing research by the USS Midway Museum, San Diego, California
**P.O.W. Network (www.pownetwork.org)

Glossary

A-4 Skyhawk	A fighter jet first produced in 1954. Two nicknames were "Scooter" and "Tinker Toy Bomber."
A-6 Intruder	An all-weather attack fighter that used radar to make accurate combat strikes in Vietnam, Lebanon, and Libya.
admiral	A very senior rank in the U.S. Navy.
air boss	The officer responsible for the safe and efficient operation of the flight deck as well as flight operations.
angled deck	The short deck on the left side of the ship that is about two-thirds the length of the ship. Used for landing aircraft.
apartheid	The basis of segregation in South Africa that ended in the early 1990s.
armada	A fleet of warships.
berthing compartment	Rooms filled with 3-high bunk beds. Some compartments contained as many as 300 bunk beds.
blisters	Large, hollow-steel containers welded onto the USS *Midway* to make it more stable in rough seas.
boot camp	Where new sailors go for several months' initial Navy training.
bow	The front of the carrier, where aircraft are launched.
bridge	Where the captain, navigator, helmsman, and others steer the ship, high above the flight deck.
brig	The ship jail, typically guarded by Marines aboard an aircraft carrier.
bulkhead	A wall within the hull of a ship.
captain	The officer responsible for a ship and its crew.
catapult	A steam-powered device to help planes take off from an aircraft carrier.
catwalk	A narrow, three-foot walkway alongside and just below the edge of the flight deck.
chief petty officer	The most senior rank an enlisted sailor can reach.
chow line	The long line leading to the galley, where food is served.
christening	A traditional ceremony marking the addition of a new ship to the fleet.
cockpit	Where the pilot and sometimes copilot sit in an aircraft.
Cold War	Nearly forty years of international tension and fears of open warfare between the U.S. and the Soviet Union.
combat information center	Where officers and sailors track aircraft-carrier operations as well as the activities of nearby ships and aircraft.

compartment	A room or designated space on a U.S. Navy ship.
corpsmen	The equivalent of nurses and medical technicians who assist ship's doctors with emergency, trauma, and preventive healthcare.
court-martial	The justice system of the military that includes trials, verdicts, and sentences.
cruise book	Similar to a high-school yearbook, issued to each sailor after a long cruise.
damage control	The department responsible for responding to all emergencies. Similar to firefighters and paramedics.
decommission	A formal ceremony when a ship is retired from active duty.
demilitarized zone	A deserted strip of land between two opposing armies.
destroyer	Fast, long-range ship armed with guided missiles.
détente	An easing of international tensions, most often used to describe the end of the Cold War.
EMCON	When a ship stops sending out radar signals to steer at night in an attempt to elude ships that may be following it.
F-4 Phantom	A fighter-bomber that saw extensive action during the Vietnam War.
F-8 Crusader	A powerful fighter jet that flew at 1.2 times the speed of sound and could climb 25,000 feet in one minute.
F-18 Hornet	All-weather strike fighter that also is flown by the Blue Angels.
fantail	The rear of the ship, just below the flight deck.
flight deck	The four-acre, solid-steel platform on the USS *Midway* where planes took off and landed.
flight surgeon	Specialized physician trained to take care of pilots, aircrews, and air-traffic controllers.
frigate	Smaller missile-equipped Navy ship that protects other ships.
galley	Where meals are prepared and served. More than 13,500 meals are served every day on an aircraft carrier.
GI Bill	Provided money for college and vocational training to veterans returning from World War II.
GM Division	The Guided Missile Division on an aircraft carrier, responsible for the missiles carried by planes.
gunnery	The responsibility for and operation of defensive guns and small cannon aboard an aircraft carrier.
hangar deck	The largest open deck on an aircraft carrier, where planes are repaired and maintained before they are lifted up to the flight deck.
Hanoi Hilton	The nickname for a large prisoner-of-war camp that held mostly American pilots near Hanoi during the Vietnam War.
hatch	Steel door that can be shut and made watertight.
homeport	The naval complex where a U.S. Navy ship is based.
island	The tall, thin structure on the side of the flight deck that contains the bridge, chartroom, primary flight control, radio antennas, and smokestacks.
kamikaze	Suicide attacks by Japanese pilots in the last days of World War II when they tried to intentionally crash into American ships.
Kent State	The site where four students protesting the Vietnam War in 1970 were shot to death by Ohio National Guardsmen.
liberty	Off-duty time spent by sailors ashore.
litter	A metal stretcher that carries the wounded.
LSO	Landing signal officer, who stands at the back of the flight deck and coaches pilots to a safe landing.

LST	Landing Ship, Tanks: ships designed to crawl up onto a beach to unload or pick up vehicles, equipment, and people.
mast	A collection of radio antennas and radar equipment above the island.
MiG	A fast and maneuverable fighter jet built by the Soviet Union and used by North Vietnamese pilots in the Vietnam War.
NATO	North Atlantic Treaty Organization, formed in 1949 by several countries to defend Europe against post-World War II expansion by the Soviet Union.
Naval Criminal Intelligence Service	The primary law-enforcement and counterintelligence arm of the U.S. Navy.
officer of the deck	The captain's representative on the bridge in the captain's absence.
Operation Desert Storm	The multination campaign to drive Iraqi troops out of occupied Kuwait in 1991.
Operation Frequent Wind	The 1975 campaign to rescue refugees during the fall of Saigon, marking the end of the Vietnam War.
Operation Frostbite	The 1946 USS *Midway* mission to the sub-Arctic to test sailors and aircraft in subfreezing weather.
ordnance	A term for rockets, bombs, missiles, and ammunition carried by a ship.
pea coat	A heavy outer coat, usually made of wool, issued to sailors.
pilothouse	The area in the front of the island that includes the navigator's station and the captain's chair, among other stations.
plane captain	A sailor responsible for making sure a plane is ready to fly before the pilot is strapped into the cockpit.
plankowner	Honorary title given to sailors who are members of the first crew of a newly commissioned ship.
pollywog	A sailor crossing the Equator on a naval ship for the first time.
poopy suit	An experimental post-World War II wetsuit worn by pilots who flew off aircraft carriers.
primary flight control	Located in the island facing the flight deck, the center that controls all flight operations. Similar to a civilian air-traffic control tower.
ready room	A compartment on an aircraft carrier reserved for pilots, where they relaxed and held meetings.
sayonara	Japanese for "goodbye."
shakedown	The first time a new ship goes to sea to determine any immediate repairs that may need to be made.
shellback	A sailor who previously has crossed the Equator on a naval ship and who initiates those crossing for the first time (see *pollywog*).
sick bay	A hospital aboard a ship.
Skyraider	The last-piston engine plane flown by Navy pilots prior to the jet age.
sponson deck	A narrow deck, more like a balcony, on the side of the hull below the flight deck.
stern	The back part of the ship.
Tonkin Gulf	The area off the Vietnamese coast where the USS *Midway* and other ships sailed in support of American troops ashore.
Truman Doctrine	On March 12, 1947, Pres. Harry Truman announced that America would supply aid to any country that resisted communism.
UNREP	Under-way replenishment, the process of resupplying Navy ships while under way in the middle of the ocean.

Index